Podcast Growth

How to Grow Your Audience

**Colin Gray, Lindsay Harris Friel, and
Matthew McLean**

Table of Contents

Introduction

"I've tried everything when it comes to growing my podcast audience, and nothing works"

Plato

373 B.C.E

A re you an obsessive podcast stats checker? Are you frustrated at the lack of growth your podcast has shown you?

Does it seem that no matter how hard you work, no matter how much great content you create, that it's still just the same small group of people listening, week after week?

Have you considered taking to social media to tell the world that podcasting is a mug's game? That it's impossible to build an audience, and that you're thinking about quitting?

Well, it looks like we got to you in the nick of time, eh?

You've picked up this book, which means you're serious about growing a fanbase around your content.

That's great news - because we're serious about helping you.

At ThePodcastHost.com, we help thousands of people to launch new podcasts every year.

No matter how many times we tell our readers and clients how easy it is to launch a podcast, many still seem surprised at the truth of this, having gone through the process themselves.

"I can't believe how simple that was!"

Making a new podcast is so easy, that when folks do it for the first time, you can bet they'll launch at least a couple more before the year is out.

But growing an audience around a podcast? Well, that isn't just so straight forward.

Sure, you can do all the groundwork pre-launch to ensure that your show is something that *can* grow.

But nothing is guaranteed in podcasting. The world doesn't owe you an audience. And "build it and they will come" only ever worked in that movie where Kevin Costner plays a baseball-loving necromancer.

You might be thinking to yourself, "Well I've tried everything already, and nothing works. My audience will never grow. Buying this stupid book was my last throw of the dice."

Well, let's make sure you're about to roll a 6.

How to Use This Book

No podcaster (not even Plato himself) ever managed to "try everything" when it comes to audience growth. There are too many things to try.

Nevertheless, we thought it'd be a great idea to pull together our favourite promotion tips and tactics, and pack them into one single book. One single book that you now own.

You don't need to do everything in this book. In fact, you probably shouldn't even try.

Every podcast is unique. Your podcast is unique. You're going to read some strategies in these pages, and think "well, that isn't relevant to me".

But, you're going to find many more that'll be extremely relevant to you. You'll be excited to try them out, and you'll be delighted at how much they move the needle.

Owning this book won't automatically grow your podcast audience - but it will give you the tools and the guidance to do it.

We've broken the book into themed chapters. Each chapter is broken down into individual strategies.

Each strategy has its own instructions, checklist, approximate time needed, and links to additional resources, if relevant.

By all means, read the book cover to cover - we hope you do. But, you can just as easily open it up at the chapter that looks the most appealing to you, and start from there.

With each growth strategy you commit to, be sure to give it the time and attention it needs to be successful. Better to do fewer things well, than to do loads of things in a half-hearted manner.

So let's dive in and get started. It's time to grow your podcast audience!

Lindsay, Matthew, & Colin

The Podcast Host Team

Enabling Your Existing Audience

"I like to listen. I have learned a great deal from listening carefully. Most people never listen."

– Ernest Hemingway

Never underestimate your current audience, the subscribers who download and listen. They can be your best PR team to spread the word about your show.

Showing appreciation for your existing audience inspires them to tell others about your podcast. Giving them tools to spread the word not only keeps messaging consistent, it helps you measure impact. Here are some methods you can use to enable your existing audience to promote your show to new potential listeners. In this section are some tools which can help.

1. **Share Buttons**

2. **Better CTAs**

3. **'How Podcasting Works' Page**

4. **Encouraging Reviews**

5. **Personal Outreach to 'True Fans'**

6. **Competitions**

7. **Creating Memorable Links**

8. **Helping Listeners Navigate Your Content**

1. Share Buttons

Make it easy for your followers to share your podcast, and they will.

You've probably seen articles online with little sharing symbols, to share the post on different kinds of social media. For example, if you click the "twitter" symbol, your browser opens up Twitter and pre-fills a tweet with the title and URL of that post.

Many Wordpress themes include these sharing buttons. You can also add sharing plugins, such as Shareaholic or Sumo. Different plugins can give you more information about what's being shared and how. Shareholic, just as an example, works with Google Analytics to track sharing data.

On your web site's episode pages, your embedded player can make your show more easily shared too. Some, such as The Smart Podcast Player and the Captivate player, include Call to Action buttons. But even a button as simple as "share" generates a link that listeners can paste into a tweet, social media post, or email to give their friends a taste of your show.

Type: Short Task

Time Required: 15 minutes to set up

Podcast Level: From the beginning

How to Do It

When you create your website, have a look at the theme. Does it let you include share buttons on posts? What social media platforms can you include? You definitely want to include Facebook and Twitter, plus whatever's relevant to your podcast topic. Pinterest and Linked In are good options. If your theme doesn't have a sharing widget that you want to use, search for a good plugin. Obviously, you should check out Shareaholic and Sumo: they're free, and help you get more data about what your audience shares and how.

Next, there's the episode player side of things. When publishing new episodes to your hosting platform, you'll use an embed code to also post the episode player on your website. Your hosting service may offer a website plug-in which helps streamline this, or you can purchase a separate plug-in, such as Pat Flynn's Smart Podcast Player.

Have a look at the podcast player you're using for your show. What kind of buttons does it have? Does it have a customizable CTA button? At the very least, you should have buttons for "subscribe" and "share."

Task List:

☐ Have a look at Shareaholic and Sumo, plus any other social sharing plugins you see.

☐ Use one of these plugins to set up social media sharing buttons on your posts

☐ Review the podcast player you use for your episodes

☐ What sharing and Call to Action buttons on your podcast player can you utilize?

Related to: Better CTAs, Organic Social Media

Further Reading:

• How To Make a Website & Blog for Your Podcast

> thepodcasthost.com/podcastwebsite

• Best Podcast Plugins for Wordpress

> thepodcasthost.com/wpplugins

• Best Podcast Players for Your Website

> thepodcasthost.com/podcastplayers

• Second Line Themes Review

> thepodcasthost.com/secondlinethemes

- WordPress Themes for Podcasting

  > thepodcasthost.com/wpthemes

2. Better CTAs

Specificity is key to a great Call to Action. How does your CTA uniquely engage your listeners? What do you want your listener to do? A specific, memorable Call to Action engages your audience and drives them in the direction you want. If your CTA includes a shortlink, it's easier for your audience to follow it.

Type: Short Task

Time Required: A few minutes per episode

Podcast Level: From the beginning

How to Do It

First, know what you want your listeners to do in each instance. Next, make it easy for them to do it. If you're sending them to a particular web page, use a shortlink to get them there. If you want them to talk about your show on social media, invent a hashtag so you can track it.

Your CTAs will totally depend on your content and motivations. But some of the most common and effective podcast CTAs we see are;

- Subscribe to the show in your listening app of choice

- Share this episode with someone you think will benefit from it

- Leave a rating and review on your listening app of choice, or in Podchaser

- Get in touch (solicit particular questions so this is more effective)

- Download a resource, sign up for something, or purchase an upgrade

Finally, include your CTAs in the show notes of each episode, in the episode outro, and if possible, linked in a button on your website podcast player.

Task List:

☐ For your next Call to Action, what do you want your listeners to do? Sum it up in a short sentence or less, such as "sign up for our email list."

☐ Look at the 'Creating Memorable Links' task, and practice making a short link.

☐ Practice your intros and outros. How can you fit your new CTA into your outros?

Related to: Creating Memorable links, Encouraging Reviews

Further Reading:

• How to Drive Action From a Podcast

  > thepodcasthost.com/driveaction

• Introducing & Ending Your Episode

  > thepodcasthost.com/outros

3. 'How Podcasting Works' Page

Inevitably, you will end up meeting someone who supports you, and is interested in your topic, but doesn't know how to listen to a podcast. If your podcast website includes a page of resources about how to listen, not only do you help them listen to your show, you might also bring some traffic to the site.

This page can include a list of instructions, a short YouTube video, and/or an embedded audio clip. People digest information in different ways. Make sure your web site has a list of links to reach your show on different listening platforms.

Type: Short Task

Time Required: About an hour

Podcast Level: from the beginning

How to Do It

Create a page on your website about how to listen to a podcast. You can explain how to listen using a smartphone, a tablet, and a computer. Emphasize that podcast listening is free. You can also explain how to listen in a car. Many cars built after 2014 have sound systems which work with smartphones, so people can listen to their own music libraries or podcasts while driving. Then, when people express interest in your podcast, but say that they don't know how to listen, you can point them to this guide.

Task List:

☐ Read our guide on "how to listen to a podcast." (linked, below)

☐ Write a short, maybe three-paragraph article, about how to listen to a podcast. Don't forget to include how to listen on a phone, a computer, and in a car. Remember to stress that it's free.

☐ Publish it on your podcast web site.

☐ Make a short link that's easy to share, such as yourpodcast.com/howtolisten.

Related to: Creating Memorable Links, Personal Outreach to 'True Fans', Helping Listeners Navigate Your Content

Further Reading:

- How To Listen To A Podcast

  > thepodcasthost.com/howtolisten

- What is a Podcast?

  > thepodcasthost.com/whatisapodcast

- Best Podcast Apps for Android and iPhone/iOS

  > thepodcasthost.com/bestpodcastapps

4. Encouraging Reviews

Nearly every podcast mentions the message "subscribe, rate and review." What if your call to action for reviews was different? Ask them to use the reviews to tell you what's most memorable about the episode they heard, for example. This makes the reviews more useful to potential listeners. Some presenters thank their reviewers in their episodes. You can also take a screenshot of any useful reviews, and post them on social media.

If someone takes the time to write out a descriptive, positive review, that's a great piece of marketing. Make those listeners feel valued, and they will advertise your podcast for you.

Type: Regular Technique

Time Required: 5 minutes per episode

Podcast Level: 4 episodes or more

How to Do It

Consider making a request for reviews in your call to action on a few episodes. Explain what reviews do for you. They can help other folks find your show, and know more about it. They also help you know what you're doing right, and where you have room to improve. Tell your audience how they can leave reviews (such as on Apple Podcasts or Podchaser).

Consider making a short YouTube video about how to do it, and share a link in your shownotes and website. Show your audience that this is a pretty fair exchange. You're providing them with great content: if they want to support your podcast, why not leave a review for you?

Sign up for a podcast analytics service, such as Chartable, Podrover, Podkite, or MyPodcastReviews. This way, you'll get an email about your reviews from every Apple Podcasts store, not only the country that you use.

Read reviews as part of your episodes. It's a good way to make your reviewers feel valued, and encourage participation. Offer an incentive when you reach a milestone number of reviews. For example, announce on your podcast that if you reach 25 reviews, you'll read some of your poetry from grade school in a special bonus episode. Or something. Make it fun!

If you offer an incentive, make sure you deliver it. Always thank your audience for their reviews.

Task List:

☐ Ask for reviews in your episode Call to Action.

☐ Sell the benefit to your listeners.

☐ Explain how to leave a review.

☐ Go to Podchaser and claim your podcast, so that you can see the reviews when they're posted.

☐ Sign up for Podrover, Chartable, Podkite, or MyPodcastReviews.

☐ If you have a friend who supports your show, ask them personally to write a review.

☐ If you get a review that's specific and stands out, take a screenshot and post it to social media.

☐ Thank your reviewers in your podcast episodes.

Related to: Personal Outreach to True Fans, Helping Navigate Your Content

Further Reading:

• How to Keep Track of Your Podcast Reviews

> thepodcasthost.com/trackyourreviews

• How to Get More Reviews on Apple Podcasts

> thepodcasthost.com/getmorereviews

5. Personal Outreach To 'True Fans'

What if you only had four listeners, but each of those listeners went around in public wearing a t-shirt saying, "I listen to (your podcast here) because it's terrific" ?

You'd have four mobile billboards, and it'd be well worth the cost of whatever t-shirts you gave them.

Word of mouth is equally effective. The more your true fans feel like they're part of your process, the more inclined they will be to keep listening, and share your show with others.

Type: Regular Technique

Time Required: 5-15 minutes per listener

Podcast Level: 10 episodes or more

How to Do It

Do you have a few friends who have listened to your podcast? Has anyone mentioned it positively on social media, or sent you good, thoughtful feedback? If they truly enjoy your show, nurture those relationships. Reach out to them. Get honest feedback from them, and use it to improve your show.

Write them a nice message. If they mentioned you on social media, send them a direct message to thank them.

If it's someone you know in real life, send them an email or chat with them personally. Keep it light and short. Ask if they'd be interested in answering a few questions about your show.

If they say yes, then ask them a couple of specifics, like "what's most memorable for you" or "how did you find out about this podcast?" Ask for suggestions about how to spread the word about your show.

Task List:

☐ Figure out who's actively listening to your show.

☐ Send them a thank you message.

☐ Ask if they'd be interested in answering some questions.

☐ Make note of their suggestions.

Related to: Organic Social Media

Further Reading:

- Creating a 'Real Life' Podcast Community

   > thepodcasthost.com/reallifecommunity

6. Competitions

Running a competition is a good way to reward your current listeners and spread the word about your show. Like a survey, it encourages participation, and shows a bit about the impact of our content on your audience. It's a more direct way to offer an incentive for paying attention to your podcast.

Type: Big Strategy

Time Required: About an hour to set up, 5-15 minutes per week to maintain for about three weeks to a month, and then about an hour to deliver the prize.

Podcast Level: At least 20 episodes

How to Do It

What's a big action that your podcast's topic includes? Is there a skill your show teaches, which you could encourage listeners to show off? Maybe listeners to your fly-fishing podcast could post pictures of their fly-tying skills on Instagram, with a hashtag that mentions your show. Then, you can search for the hashtag to find all of the entries, and pick the best fly.

An easier way to do this is to remove the element of judgment, and randomly select a winner. Invite your listeners to respond to a particular call to action, such as signing up for your mailing list or something, within a particular date window. Then, use a tool such as Google's Random Number Generator, to pick a winner (i.e., if the tool picks "four," the fourth person to enter is the winner).

Make sure that you come up with a prize which you can deliver easily. A digital prize is the safest bet. If it's something physical, you may need to ship it to the other side of the world!

Task List:

☐ Decide on a prize which you can easily deliver.

☐ Decide how to have the competitors submit their entries. Email? Social media posts with a hashtag?

☐ Announce the competition on your podcast and social media. Make sure you let them know when the deadline is.

☐ Remind your audience (on social media and in your CTA) about the competition for 3-4 subsequent episodes.

☐ Close the competition, announcing the end on social media.

☐ Select your winner.

☐ Deliver the prize to them.

Related to: Surveys, Personal Outreach to 'True Fans'

7. Creating Memorable Links

Short, clear URLs are easier to say, remember, share and use. When you're creating your website, you can edit URLs to simplify them. Better yet, use a link shortening system. When you're providing links to surveys, forms, or bonus content, use a short link tool like PrettyLinks to keep your link easy to share. What's easier, yourpodcast.com/episodes/season1/episode10/survey,   or yourpodcast.com/survey?

Type: Regular Technique

Time Required: 5 minutes to set up, less time to use routinely

Podcast Level: From day one

How to Do It

When you create a URL for a page or post in Wordpress, the title of that page or post is the last part of the URL, by default. However, you can edit it to make it shorter.

Another option is to use a link shortener. This is a tool which lets you create a short URL that will redirect to the page you want. You may have seen these in social media posts. They often look like bit.ly/title. However, you can make a link shortening tool work harder for you, by picking one that gives you information.

PrettyLinks, for example, will provide some tracking data. It's a plugin that you can add to your Wordpress site.

Using a tool like PrettyLinks means that, when you include a link in a CTA, it's easy for you to say on your episodes. It's also easy for your audience to remember, and use.

Task List:

☐   Add the PrettyLinks plugin to your website.

☐   Use it every time you need to link a special page.

Related to: Organic Social Media, Advertising Your Podcast, Surveying Your Audience, Competitions, Personal Outreach to "True Fans"

Further Reading:

- How to Drive Action from a Podcast

  > thepodcasthost.com/driveaction

8. Helping Listeners Navigate Your Content

If you're blessed with lots of fresh, original podcast ideas, great! Keep up the good work. However, when your listeners share your content with a friend, this new friend might not know where to begin. Organizing your episodes, your web site, and your topics gives new listeners a point of entry, and seasoned listeners an easier way to share it.

Type: Ongoing Strategy

Time Required: A few minutes to an hour per week.

Podcast Level: From day one

How to Do It

Think about how your podcast topic can be divided down into smaller categories. For example, if your podcast is about dogs, you might have episodes about different breeds, care and feeding, veterinary concerns, and so on.

Within those concepts, there are sub-categories. "Different breeds" can include big dogs, little dogs, medium-sized dogs, and then subcategories from there. "Little dogs" can include chihuahuas, papillons, and so on. If someone recommended your dog podcast as a great resource for information about food for shih tzus, would the new listener be able to find that information easily?

There are a few ways to break down your ideas and organize them so listeners can navigate your content easily. You can plan, record and publish your podcast in seasons. You can organize and set up your website by topic and sub-category. You can also create a guide or 'Start Here' page on your website to help new folks find what they want to hear first. This page makes it easier for your audience to share your show, and for new folks to find and pay attention to it.

Podcasting in seasons doesn't have to be as literal as "fall 2020" or "spring 2021." Think about focusing on one broader part of your topic for a set number of episodes, call that a season, then another topic for a set number of episodes, and so on. You can also give yourself a break between seasons to generate new ideas, or just recharge. Season-based podcasting can help you plan your content calendar, which in turn helps you post consistently. It also helps your listeners know what to expect, which makes you more of a habit.

In terms of your website design, you can set up categories for different types of posts, and then tags for details. For example, you can have one category of posts for text and photo blog posts, and another category for podcast episodes. If you've been blogging for a while and want to add podcasting to your content strategy, categories are a good way to let the established blog posts and the podcast episode posts have their own focus.

With categories, sub-categories and smaller details, you can see how this works. For example, if you have a category of podcast episode posts about "dog breeds," you can have sub-categories of episodes where you've talked about shih tzus, newfoundlands, and so on. If you have an episode about dog diet, you can have different categories for different types of food or dietary concerns. If your episode which focused on shih tzus briefly touched on grooming, you can tag it with "grooming."

Think of each category as a nesting doll, with your topic and episodes nested inside it.

Some website themes make categories and tags easy. On Wordpress, the Elegant themes help you set up categories and tags. Divi is an Elegant theme which can show lists of posts by category. The WP bakery page builder can show a grid of blog posts, categorized. List Category Posts is a plugin that will show a list of posts by category or tag, and it's free.

If your web site includes a guide page, this can make new listeners feel welcome, and reward seasoned listeners for sharing, by making it simple. Think of your guide page as a party host who welcomes you, and points out the snack table, the drinks table, and the conversation lounge.

Tasks:

☐ Look over your podcast topics, and what you talked about.

☐ Write out a list of your podcast topic categories.

☐ Try Divi, WPBakery, and List Category Posts. See which is best for your needs.

☐ Create a guide page which shows new listeners where to start

☐ Make a list of seasons, and a list of categories.

☐ Include a 'Start Here' link on your homepage.

Further reading:

• Divi, a Wordpress Theme and Page Builder

> thepodcasthost.com/divi

• WPBakery Page Builder for Wordpress

> thepodcasthost.com/WPBakery

• List Category Posts for Wordpress

> thepodcasthost.com/listcategoryposts

Growing Your Audience by Knowing Your Audience

How to Run a Listener Survey

"If we knew what we were doing, it wouldn't be called research."

-Albert Einstein

The more you know about your audience, the better you'll be able to connect with them, and make your podcast better. One of the best ways to get to know your audience is through going directly to them with a survey. This chapter shows you how to maximise the impact of this strategy.

Why Survey Your Listeners?

When your audience feels that they're important, they're more likely to continue paying attention. Surveying your current audience builds trust, and helps you shape your future content.

Type: Big Strategy

Time Required: An hour to set up, three episodes of your podcast to share in your CTA or on social media, and an hour to analyze survey responses.

Podcast Level: 10 episodes, or once your workflow is established

How to Do It

It's important to ask yourself why you're doing this, so you can find out what you want to discover. What can you get out of this survey? You can find out what your audience enjoys about your show, and what they don't. You can also gather suggestions for future content. With a prize drawing, you can gather email addresses for a mailing list (with their consent, of course).

Knowing what kind of people (age, demographic region, level of education, and so on) are paying attention to your work can help you tailor your content. It can also help you to fit your advertising to your audience and people like them. If you plan to host live recordings or other events in the future, this will help as well.

Surveys can include some general questions about age, nationality, gender identity, and basic interests, where they're relevant to your show's topic.

Think about how your show's presented, and how you structure it. Do you have recurring segments? Do you turn the mic on, talk for an hour, and then stop? Do you have a co-host, or interview guests? Ask what your listeners think about what you currently do, and what they'd like to have you do in the future.

Some of the reasons that people listen to your show may surprise you. Maybe they have no interest in your topic, but your voice and cadence helps them relax or even sleep. Asking your listeners what they get out of your show can help you figure out what to highlight, and what to set aside.

Ask what they do while listening. How does your show help them do it? Is there something which they wouldn't be able to do (tolerate a long day of data entry? Are they homesick for your region, maybe?) without your podcast? Likewise, is there an aspect of your podcast they could do without?

26

Here's a tricky facet of looking after your listeners. When it comes to your podcast topic, is there something with which they struggle? For example, if your podcast is about baking, are some of your listeners having trouble with separating eggs?

Open-ended questions can yield surprising results.

There will always be aspects of your podcast that someone doesn't like. Some of these will be spots you can improve. Others are things which make your show unique, and you should keep them.

For example, if the presenter has a lisp, and it drives some of the audience crazy, the presenter can do tongue-twisters to improve their enunciation. Topic, presentation and confidence often far outweigh a speech impediment. Jonathan Ross still has a career, right?

Encourage your audience to be honest, don't take negative criticism personally, and fix what you can. What you can't fix, consider part of your show's unique charm.

If or when you get negative comments, watch to see if it's isolated, unfounded, or just someone trolling you. For example, there's a big difference between, "the female presenter sounds shrill," and "there was a tinny timbre in the voice which put me off."

You should definitely ask your audience how they found you. Traditional media doesn't often recognize indie podcasters, and charts of podcast directories tend to show celebrity podcasts more often than not. Knowing how your current listeners found your podcast can help you target future advertising efforts.

Now that you've figured out what to know and why, and how to ask, it's time for the part where the rubber meets the road. You've decided what survey tool is right for you, what questions you want to ask, and how you want to execute your survey. Start typing up your questions, and sharing them with your audience.

Task List:

☐ Write down a list of goals for the survey (what you hope to learn).

☐ Have a look at some survey tools, such as SurveyMonkey, PollDaddy, or Google Forms, to find out what's best for you.

☐ Have a look at a tool like PrettyLinks. This will help you make a short, memorable URL to include in your call to action.

☐ Decide how long you want the survey to run. You should have enough time to mention the survey in at least 3 of your episodes.

☐ Think up some general questions about demographics to add to your survey.

☐ Come up with a few (2-4) survey questions about your show's format, such as episode length, format type, or whatever else comes to mind.

☐ Ask if there are segments they prefer.

☐ Ask if there are segments they tune out, ignore or skip.

☐ Ask what aspect of your podcast's topic they find difficult, or what they do while listening.

☐ What does your podcast help them do better?

☐ Ask about how they first heard about your show. What motivated them to click on the link and start listening?

☐ Enter your questions into the survey tool of your choice.

☐ Make a shortlink to the survey that's easy to remember and share.

☐ Promote your survey to your listeners on social media, on your podcast website, and in your call to action, for at least three subsequent episodes.

☐ Leave the survey up and running for as long as it takes for your listeners to have heard it in at least 3 of your podcast episode calls to action.

☐ Close the survey, and tabulate the results. Look for patterns. What do you notice?

☐ Does this change your picture of your audience avatar? What ideas does it give you for changes to make?

Related To: Enabling Your Existing Audience, Helping Others To Help Yourself, Gaining New Visibility, Advertising Your Podcast, Being Found Easily

Further Reading:

- Growing Your Podcast With An Audience Survey

    > thepodcasthost.com/howtosurvey

- Podcast Formats: The Complete Guide

    > thepodcasthost.com/formatguide

- Creating a 'Real Life' Podcast Community

    > thepodcasthost.com/reallifecommunity

- How To Deal With Criticism

    > thepodcasthost.com/criticism

- Podcast Discoverability: How Do Listeners *Actually* Find Their Favourite Shows?

    > thepodcasthost.com/discovery

Running Live Events

"I've got a dream too, but it's about singing and dancing and making people happy. That's the kind of dream that gets better, the more people you share it with. And, well, I've found a whole bunch of friends who have the same dream. And it kind of makes us like a family."

– Kermit The Frog

A live event is a great way to get your audience excited about your podcast. They may bring friends that are new to your work, which can expand your audience. Podcast episodes that are recorded live can seem more exciting, because the audience is part of the experience. If your venue is a place that has its own following (such as a bar, cafe or cabaret space), you may attract people who are new to the podcast as well. All in all, this is a good way to inject some excitement into your podcast and grow your audience.

1. **How to Organise a Live Event**

2. **Create a Local Podcasters' Group**

3. **Promoting Events**

1. How to Organise a Live Event

Booking a space and recording an episode with a live audience is more work, sure, but the results are worth it. You'll end up with an episode with the pizazz of audience reaction, and you can get your audience telling others about your show.

Type: Big Strategy

Time Required: At least three weeks, up to six, to plan, promote, and execute

Podcast Level: 10 episodes or more

How to Do It

If you've been running your show for a while, and have a following, find out what geographic region has the most downloads. Hopefully, this is near where you live.

Find a venue that you can rent, or speak to the proprietor about using it for an event. If it's a cafe or bar, they may be willing to let you host for free. Some bars and cafes which host live music events have their own sound equipment, and will let you host an event there in exchange for paying their sound engineer. Churches often have community meeting rooms, or your local community centre may have a space as well.

Some venues will let you use their space in exchange for promotion. Whether you pay to book the space or not, it's good form to mention the venue and talk about it as positively as possible. What can you do for them? Hopefully, this means you'll bring in paying customers and promote their pub/cafe/ etc. to new people. When you talk with them, think in terms of how you can affect their business or organization in a positive way.

Your field recording setup probably doesn't have much in the way of speakers. You'll need to know if the venue has speakers you can plug into, or bring your own, to ensure the audience can hear you.

Charging admission to your live event is a tricky question. Are you paying a sound engineer? Renting the space? Does your podcast include performers who you want to compensate? If your audience is dedicated and local, they might not mind paying an admission fee. If you're still in your early growth stages, you may want to consider making the event free to attend.

Make sure that the audience knows you're recording a live episode (it should be fairly obvious) so they're encouraged to react audibly.

You may want to consider selling merchandise at the event, to offset any costs and generate more interest. This is something you should consider after you've hosted one or more live events, and have experience under your belt. If so, have a friend help with setting up a merch table and running it, so you can concentrate on recording, presenting, and other aspects of the event. Likewise, if you're charging admission, have a friend handle this for you. Make sure they have a bank of small bills to make change, or be able to take card purchases.

Think of your audience as guests. Greet them personally if you can.

While this episode will definitely be unique (no two live shows are ever alike), you might want to think about having a guest to add interest. For example, if the event is in a city you're not familiar with, consider inviting someone local to chat about the town with you, as part of the show.

Back up your recording one more time than you think you need to, just in case a memory card or hard drive is lost in transportation. When all is edited and polished, you'll have unique and exciting content, and you'll have generated more word of mouth.

Task List:

☐   Find out where most of your subscribers and fans live. Check your media host's downloads, or survey your audience.

☐ Look for a few venues around that area (cafes, bars, community centres, church rec rooms, and so on).

☐ Ask proprietors about hosting a live podcast recording in their space.

☐ Make sure that it has enough electrical outlets to support your equipment.

☐ Plan the event to occur on a date that's far enough in the future that you can mention it in the CTA of at least three episodes of your podcast.

☐ Practice setting up and packing up your recording gear in advance.

☐ Promote your live event on social media, on your website, and especially in the call to action of your podcast.

☐ Show up at least an hour before your event starts, to set up your gear.

☐ After the show ends, get your gear packed up as quickly as possible, so that nothing goes missing.

☐ Thank your audience for coming. Thank the proprietor, face to face and on your podcast.

☐ Remember the campsite rule: leave the place in better shape than you found it. Clean up after yourself, put chairs away if necessary, and so on.

☐ Polish up your audio and share it with your audience.

Related to: Helping Others To Help Yourself, Enabling Your Existing Audience, Attending Live Events, Growing Your Audience By Knowing Your Audience, Merchandise, Organic Social Media

Further Reading:

- How To Podcast from An Event

> thepodcasthost.com/podcastfromevent

- Why Record Your Podcast Outdoors?

  > thepodcasthost.com/recordingoutdoors

- Examples of Simple Podcasting Setups

  > thepodcasthost.com/perfectsetup

- Live Broadcasting

  > thepodcasthost.com/livepod

2. Create a Local Podcasters' Group

Admit it: you can always use the support of your colleagues. Whether other people who make podcasts have more experience, less experience, or different kinds of experience, there's always inspiration and strength that comes from being involved with other podcasters. Creating a local group takes some work, and a long period of time, but in the end, you can build community, grow your show, and help others.

Type: Regular technique

Time Required: Put an hour a week into promoting it and an hour for each meeting.

Podcast Level: 10 episodes, or when your workflow is established and comfortable

How to Do It

You probably participate in an online community of podcasters already. If you don't, you certainly can. You can also survey your audience to find out where your listeners are, and what percentage of them are podcasters themselves.

Find a local coffee shop, pub, or community centre that will let a few people sit around and chat over a beverage for a while. Plan a recurring meeting, brainstorm some discussion topics, and promote the meeting to your friends and followers.

It can be handy to set a topic in advance for each meeting. This can encourage people to turn up.

You can also create meetups online. This gives you the option to meet people anywhere in the world, but removes the impact of face to face interaction.

Whichever you choose, be open to listening, use your best manners, and empower others to do the same.

Task List:

- ☐ Decide if you want the meeting to be virtual or actual (online or in-person).

- ☐ Find an online platform to use, or a venue to meet up in.

- ☐ Arrange a time and date.

- ☐ Mention the meeting on your social media, and in your podcast's call to action. You want to be able to do this for at least three episodes of your podcast.

- ☐ Set a topic (or topics) in advance.

- ☐ Get to the meeting early, greet people when they arrive.

- ☐ If you meet in a physical location, make sure that you leave it clean, and in better shape than you found it.

Related to: Enabling Your Existing Audience, Attending Live Events, Being Found Easily, Online Communities, Growing Your Audience By Knowing Your Audience, Gaining New Visibility,

Further Reading:

- Building a Community

  > hepodcasthost.com/buildingcommunity

- Creating a 'Real Life' Podcast Community

  > thepodcasthost.com/reallifecommunity

3. Promoting Events

Live events are great, but not if people don't know about them. How do you invite people and get them to come out?

Type: Short Task (recurring)

Time Required: 15 minutes

Podcast Level: As soon as you have a live event to promote

How to Do It

People need to find out about your live event at least three times in order for it to stick. Not only do they need to know where and when it's happening, they need to know why, and what's in it for them. How will your live event add value to their lives? In what way is it better than staying home with the cat? Take some time and ask yourself these things.

What could be some obstacles to attending your live event? Is the place hard to find, or not handicapped-accessible? Is it on a night when people have to get up for work or school in the morning? Figure out how to circumvent these obstacles. This way you'll make it easier to attend, even if it's just a tip like, "use the entrance on the side street, not the front entrance."

Then, when you share the event with your audience, they'll be more inclined to join you.

Task List:

☐ Make a list of reasons to come to your live event.

☐ Figure out how those obstacles can be navigated.

☐ Craft an invitation. Include the place and time, what you're going to do (is this a live episode recording, or a casual meetup?), and what's unique about it (will there be special guests? Are you meeting in a haunted spaghetti restaurant?)

☐ Include this in your episode's Call To Action and your social media posts.

☐ Make an announcement as a post on your website, with all the information: time, date, place, and how to get there. Include directions, parking info, and the cost of admission, if any.

☐ Use PrettyLinks or another link-shortening tool to make a shortlink. This will be easier for you to include in a Call To Action or social media post.

☐ Give yourself enough lead time that you can mention this event in at least three episodes of your podcast.

Related to: Enabling Your Existing Audience, Attending Live Events, Helping Others To Help Yourself, Looking After Your Listeners, Organic Social Media

Further Reading:

• Building a Community

  > thepodcasthost.com/buildingcommunity

• Creating a 'Real Life' Podcast Community

  > thepodcasthost.com/reallifecommunity

• How to Drive Action from Your Podcast

  > thepodcasthost.com/driveaction

Being Found Easily

"If you build it, they will come." - Spooky field voices.

But only if you build it to be found...

A lot of growth tactics concentrate on going out there into the world and shouting about what you've done. They're about finding people, and making them aware of your work. But, there's a huge opportunity for growth when you flip that on its head. Instead of going out and finding THEM, what about making it easier for them to find YOU?

There's a lot you can do to make yourself more easily found. In simple terms, it's all about creating your content with the listener, with Google and with the podcast directories in mind. Then, you apply a few SEO tactics that help them all find and understand you.

For me, this is something to be done in the first stages of audience growth, because it's very much a long term play. It doesn't work overnight. But, if you build audience-centric SEO into your content, right from the start, then you create a huge advantage in the long term.

One reason for this is because text is still the largest search medium. So many more people search on Google, every day, than in Apple Podcasts, Spotify or any other podcast directory. Some of them are podcast listeners already, and they'll find you that way. But many, many more haven't ever listened to a podcast, so they'd never find you in any podcast directory. Instead, they'll find your website content, read a few valuable tips in your shownotes, and think: "Oh, there's an audio player here... wonder what that does? <Click> Ooooohhhh...how do I subscribe to this?!"

No longer are you fighting for existing podcast listeners. Instead, you're expanding the podcast listening audience, reaching *everyone* with an internet connection.

Thankfully, those techniques that work to help you be found in Google - they work in very much the same way for podcast directories. And even better, these aren't techie hacks that mean nothing to the listener. Much of it is about making your content even more clear and more valuable for the listener. After all, that's what Google wants, and Google's smart. It can tell!

So, how does it work?

The first step in this is creating content that people really want, by answering questions they're actually asking. That means you'll appear for those searches, you'll appeal to the listener, and it makes them more likely to share it with others. I'll show you how to find out what people are searching for in your niche through a range of tools and tactics.

Next, we'll explore how to include that information in your podcast episode data, and on your website. Those are the tactics that help make it obvious to Google, the podcast directories, and your listener (!) what problem you're solving. If the search engines know what you're solving, then they show it to the listener. And if it's obvious to the listener, then they're much more likely to click subscribe. That's one big path to sustainable growth. So, let's get started!

1. **Ask Your Whole Audience**
2. **Ask One of Your Audience**
3. **Keyword Research**
4. **Question Research**
5. **Episode Titles**
6. **The Rest of the Page**

1. Ask Your Whole Audience

The first step powers the rest of this chapter and is pretty darn obvious. But, it's so often missed by Podcasters:

Ask your existing audience what they're struggling with!

I'm sure you're thinking: "I already know what they're thinking!" But nothing beats going straight to the horse's mouth.

I've lost count of the number of times I've been surprised by a question I never considered, a barrier I've never encountered, or even a new angle on an existing topic. The only way to create content that really resonates with your audience, and matches what they're searching for, is to talk to them.

The aim here is to unearth the questions they're asking right now, and the language they ask them in. Your biggest problem as an expert is that you know too much! An example from our area is the question:

How do you upload a podcast to iTunes?

There are two reasons we totally missed this in the early days. First, you don't upload a podcast to iTunes at all. It's a mistaken assumption! And second, iTunes doesn't even really exist any more. It's Apple Podcasts! As an expert, you don't even consider some of the questions that are really misconceptions, or in the wrong terminology. That's why you have to speak to your audience. Only then will you hear what's really on their minds, and how they ask it. The "how they ask" is vital. You need to communicate the question in their way, first, so they know you're offering the answer they seek.

Once you have your set of questions, written in their language, you can then move on with the rest of this chapter.

What if you don't have an existing audience? Then find them out there in the world! Dive into online communities that cover your topic. Go to live events in your industry. Join the clubs that your audience are members of. It's your job to find your potential listeners, and join them wherever they hang out. This doesn't only help with sourcing questions, too. It'll tie into many more of the techniques in this book.

Type: Regular Technique

Time Required: 2 to 4 hours per month

Podcast Level: 5 episodes

How to Do It

This is something I recommend working on for a few hours per month, but it's likely you're doing it on a regular basis, without even thinking about it. Here's how to build it into your regular routine:

1. Think about the most common questions that come your way. What do clients, customers or listeners ask you first? Then, what less common things do they ask once you get to know them?

2. Proactively seek questions. Ask on your podcast and on social media, what are people struggling with? What's on their mind? What's holding them back in achieving their goals, related to your topic?

3. Make it really, really easy for people to respond. One possibility is a very simple survey. Perhaps a page on your website with just one text field on it: "What are you struggling with? Write in below and we'll answer it on the show." Create a shortlink for this through Prettylinks or a similar tool, so it's super-easy to direct people towards the survey.

Task List:

☐ Spend 30 minutes thinking about the questions you've been asked. Write down the top 10 questions.

☐ Ask on social media and on the podcast: What are you struggling with right now?

☐ Make it easy for people to answer: potentially a survey & shortlink to it.

☐ Start planning content that really answers those top 10 questions.

Related to: Enabling Your Existing Audience, Helping Yourself by Helping Others, Growing Your Audience By Knowing Your Audience

2. Ask One of Your Audience

If you want to make sure you're really creating the right content for your audience, then speak to them directly! In the previous task, we spoke to them en-masse, but this time we want to go deep with just one or two people.

Type: Regular Technique

Time Required: 1 or 2 hours per month

Podcast Level: 5 episodes

How to Do It

If you're just starting out, you might need to get out to some events or join some communities to find them. If you already have an audience, then pick out a few people from your mailing list, or from your Twitter audience, and ask them to jump on a Zoom chat. If you have personal friends that are in your target audience, buy them a coffee.

It only takes 3 or 4 of these a month to stay 'in the know'. You'll be so in touch with your audience's needs that you can't fail to create content that speaks right to their greatest pains. That's what draws people in and compels them to share it with others.

Scheduling tools make this really easy. Set up some meeting slots using a tool like Book Like a Boss. Then, send the link to those you pick out. This process saves hours in arranging your meetings.

Task List:

☐ Just starting: Find those real people, and have in-person conversations – go to clubs, join communities, go to events. Get in conversations!

☐ Established: Pick some random people from your email list or social following. Get in touch and book them, using Book Like a Boss.

Related To: Enabling Your Existing Audience, Growing Your Audience by Knowing Your Audience

Further Reading:

- Book Like a Boss Review and signup link

  > thepodcasthost.com/booking

3. Keyword Research for Surfacing & Prioritising Topics

Okay, we've covered the human angle. We've talked to real people to surface the big pains in our niche. Now, let's combine that data with some specific keyword research tools to dig much, much deeper. This means taking one idea for a question and using technology to find everything related to it. You won't believe how many exciting insights this uncovers!

Even better, keyword research really is key (pun intended...) in creating content that's *worthwhile*. Just a few minutes of research can make all the difference between a post that languishes in obscurity, and a post that attracts thousands of readers.

Type: Regular technique

Time Required: Fifteen minutes per episode

Podcast Level: From the beginning

How to Do It

After the first two tactics in this chapter, you'll now have a list of killer questions in your pocket. That's a great start, but it can also serve as ammo to uncover so much more.

First, let's use a tool you see in Google search every day. To find it, type in a basic question about your topic. In the search results, usually at the bottom of the 1st page, a section labelled, "People also ask," will appear.

So, for example, if you type in, "how can I learn fly fishing?" then the "People also ask" feature comes up with, "Where can I learn fly fishing?" and "What's the difference between fly fishing and regular fishing?" This pops up because Google knows intimately what people's search habits are. This means that when someone types in that first question, they often type in one of those other questions next. Google knows what the world is asking! Now you've got at least two (if not more) new topics for future episodes.

Next, we can dive into a specific keyword research tool to get even more insight and to begin to prioritise. The Google AdWords Keyword Planner is one of the best, and it's free! Load up the tool, using the link below, and use the "search for new keywords" tool. Type in one of your main keywords or keyphrases, and then dive in. Browse through, looking for topics.

For example, if I type "Podcasting" we see: Podcast app (one of the biggest searches), best podcasts, podcast equipment, and podcast directory. If I dig a bit deeper, I find podcast hosting sites, create a podcast, podcast gear, and podcast recorder.

The best thing about Google's keyword planner is that it does your prioritisation for you! Look at the number of monthly searches, right next to each keyword. That shows you how popular that topic is, so tackle the most popular first! Even better, take your top 10 questions, from the previous section, and type in the main keywords from them. This shows you which questions are most commonly searched, and so, which ones to start with.

There are paid tools to help with this too. We use Semrush right now, which is really good, but Ahrefs is a very popular alternative. Warning: these tools are expensive, but it's because of the value they offer in ensuring you spend time writing about the right things, and grow a big audience as a result.

These tools offer extra data, like competition and how difficult it'll be to rank for a certain keyword or phrase. They can also show what your competitors are doing well for, so you can get extra insight into topics that you should cover too. ..

Task List:

☐ Search on Google, using questions around your topic.

☐ Make note of the questions that come up under "People also ask."

☐ Get into the Google Keyword Planner and try out your niche keywords.

☐ Use the Search for new keywords using a phrase, website or category option.

☐ Delve in – go really deep, try different variations.

☐ Note down the phrases, the words, the language that pops up, and use them to inspire and title future content.

☐ Prioritise your next 10 episode topics by search volume from Google's keyword tool.

☐ Consider a paid tool like Semrush or Serpstat for extra insight and competitor research.

Related to: Personal Outreach to 'True Fans', Organic Social Media, Online Communities

Further Reading:

• Keyword SEO for Podcasters

> thepodcasthost.com/keywordseo

4. Question Research

In the previous task, we looked at a few tools tailored to keyword research. This time around, we're going longer: looking at tools which unearth not just words, but entire questions. This builds on your personal research from earlier in the book, by looking at what people on the web are asking more widely. Here are the tools we'll be using to unearth more questions to answer:

- AnswerThePublic

- Twitter – search keyword + ? or a question word (what, how, when)

- Quora

- Buzzsumo, to unearth what's shared a lot in your niche

Type: Regular Technique

Time Required: 2 to 4 hours per month

Podcast Level: From the beginning

How To Do It

Questions are great. More and more, users are typing full questions into Google, rather than single words or phrases. Google can see this, and loves it when you answer them directly. If it's obvious what you're answering, they'll direct ever more users to your answers.

On top of that, when you think in questions, you tend to solve a real problem. Solve someone's problem and they'll be a loyal listener for life! That's what powers real audience growth. So, where do we find these questions?

"Answer the Public" is a great resource for this. It's a website which is similar, in a way, to the keyword tool discussed earlier, but it's designed to surface every possible question around a keyword or keyphrase. Type in your keyword - eg. podcasting - and you'll see a huge list of questions. You'll see them grouped by type - why? what? who? - and you can refine it along the way. Wait till you see the questions that you never even considered!

Next, let's use social media, and Twitter in particular, to see what people are asking, right now! The technique is simple: type in your keyword AND a ? or a question word. This prompts twitter to surface all tweets that ask a question related to your topic. Eg.

- Podcast AND?

- meditation AND how

- Nutrition AND what

Another great resource is Quora, an entire website of questions! Type in your topic, or related keywords, and see what questions pop up.

Finally, try Buzzsumo to see what type of content is really resonating with your niche right now. Type in your keywords and it'll surface the most shared content in your niche. This should give you ideas on what people are really connecting with right now.

Task List:

☐ Pick at least one of the above tools and go in deep on it.

☐ Try all your topic or keyword variations and see if you can write down at least 10 of the most common questions people are asking.

☐ Use these as your next set of podcast topics and you'll increase your search visibility by a huge amount.

☐ Bonus points: use the Google keyword tool from above to check search volume and prioritise your questions.

Related to: Organic Social Media, Helping Yourself by Helping Others

5. Episode Titles

We know, now, that we're creating the right content. Next, how do we make sure that Google spots it? How do we make sure we have the best chance of ranking first in Google for that topic? The first step is choosing the perfect page and episode title.

Type: Regular Technique

Time Required: 15 minutes per episode

Podcast Level: From the beginning

How To Do It

One of the biggest growth mistakes podcasters make is wasting space in their episode titles. Take this, for example: Episode 123: Talking to Colin Gray from Alitu About Podcasting.

Think about this from a 'search' perspective. Is anyone typing in 'Episode 123'? Is anyone typing in 'Colin Gray from Alitu'? No! They're typing in questions. They're searching for solutions! So, prioritise that in your titles.

Your title should make it really obvious what problem you're solving. As we said, Google loves questions, so the best solution is to ask the question in your title.

For example, "What are the best...?" "When should I...?" "Where should I...?" Or, you can use teaching words like 'How to' or 'When to'.

Next, make sure the most common keywords or phrases are in there. For example, I found "Podcast App," earlier. A great title would be, "What's the Best Podcast App for iPhones?"

Or if we were to rework that terrible title above, how about this:

How can a Podcast Help to Grow your Sales, with Colin Gray from Alitu.

Question and problem up front, then the other info if you really want it. And get rid of episode numbers altogether. Remember, the aim is to attract searches on the web as well as your podcast app. No-one cares about episode numbers on the web, and all of the top podcast apps add episode numbers automatically.

When people see the question they're asking, right there in the title, they won't hesitate to click. And when it works well for searchers, it works well for Google, so they'll rank you accordingly. Once you're ranking high in text search, you enter a whole new league of audience growth.

Task List:

☐ Create an episode title that makes it totally obvious what problem you're solving, or what question you're answering.

☐ Include your top keyword or keyphrase in the title, as close to the start of it as you can.

☐ Right now, go back to your most recent 3 episodes and change the titles based on these rules.

Further Reading:

• Keyword SEO for Podcasters

> thepodcasthost.com/keywordseo

6. The Rest of the Page

Our title is now spot on. What about the rest of the page? It's vital to make it as clear as possible, to Google, what the content is all about. That means following a set of SEO guidelines to signal what the topic is and what questions you answer. Let's take a look at exactly what to do, on the page, to stand the best chance of ranking high in search.

Type: Regular Technique

Time Required: 30 minutes per episode

Podcast Level: From the beginning

How to Do It

Here are the main SEO rules to follow when creating show notes for your next episode:

Create a title that makes it totally obvious what problem you're solving, or what question you're answering. Include your top keyword or keyphrase in the title, as close to the start of it as you can. The title is the #1 signal to Google on what the page covers.

Next, consider the headers inside the article. These are big signals to Google, too. Make sure to include the main question in at least one header, inside the page. I often find the last paragraph is a good place, with something like:

Summary: What are the best Podcast Apps?

Include variations of your keywords and phrases in other headers too, where it makes sense.

Then, in the main content itself, make sure to include a variation of your main question once or twice, and sprinkle your main keywords and phrases evenly around the article.

Remember, don't shoehorn them in, it needs to stay readable. But it's often possible to get your main keywords and phrases in quite a few times in a really natural way.

Next, fill out your image alt tags, and include keywords where possible. Alt tags are vital anyway, to help visually impaired users, but you can often include images where the alt tags will naturally include keywords, and still be really useful. For example, in an article where we review the Samson Q2U microphone, we'll include a picture of the mic itself. This means we can include the alt tag which describes the image, but also includes our keyword: "The Samson Q2U microphone".

Use the Yoast SEO plugin to evaluate how well you're doing with this. It'll give you a score based on how often your keywords appear in the title, the headers and the content. It'll even tell you how well it's distributed, or whether you've gone overboard.

Make your show notes page at least 400 words long, preferably longer. Check out our show notes guide, linked to below, for great things to include which will help lengthen it out and make it more valuable to listeners. This will help ensure you're adding useful content, not just padding.

Finally, fill out a good Meta description for the page using Yoast SEO. These are the two sentences that appear below the page title in search results. A good meta description can really boost the number of people that click on your article in search. And the more people that click, the more Google sees your article as a great resource. That feeds back into their algorithm and can lead to higher rankings.

This is a slow burn, but trust me, do this for every episode over a few months and you'll start to grow your traffic over the long term, in a way that few other techniques can achieve.

Task List:

☐   Go back to your most recent episode, and apply these rules to your show notes page.

☐ Then follow the rules for all future episodes.

☐ Include the question text, or the keywords, in the main text of the post.

☐ Include the question text, or the keywords, in at least one subheader.

☐ Images – include the keywords in the alt text, in a natural way.

☐ In the main text, use some variations of the keywords or questions.

☐ Meta description – fill this out with a compelling reason to click through to your page.

☐ Use Yoast SEO to assess how well you're doing.

Further Reading:

• Creating Great Podcast Shownotes: What Format Should I Follow?

   > thepodcasthost.com/shownotes

• Keyword SEO for Podcasters

   > thepodcasthost.com/keywordseo

Podcast Directories

"People don't buy goods and services. They buy relations, stories and magic."

-Seth Godin

You want to make sure your podcast can be found anywhere that people listen to podcasts. This means submitting it to a few different destinations. The good news is that you only have to do it once per directory. Also, most podcast listening apps on the market pull all their data from Apple Podcasts, so simply submitting your show there will automatically put your show in the majority of listening apps.

However, some other big directories have their own processes. We want to make sure your show is available everywhere it can be, so that it's truly optimised for growth.

When you upload your podcast sound files and art to your media hosting provider, that's where the podcast "lives". The RSS feed - a unique URL you'll get from your media host - is like a telephone line out from the files' home. To connect your episodes to podcast listening directories, you have to give them your RSS feed, and they have to accept it.

Processes can vary slightly from directory to directory, but all follow the same principles, and aren't difficult to do.

These days, most media hosts even have a section titled 'Destinations', 'Directories' or something similar, where you can submit to these places at the click of a button. If you don't see these options in your hosting provider dashboard though, then this chapter will run you through it.

1. **Apple Podcasts (formerly iTunes)**

2. **Spotify**

3. **Google Podcasts**

4. **Stitcher**

5. **TuneIn**

6. **Amazon Alexa/Echo**

7. **RadioPublic**

8. **Podchaser**

1. Apple Podcasts (iTunes)

Apple is the tech giant which brought us the iPod, which in turn popularised the term "podcast." Most podcast listening apps (other than the ones mentioned in this chapter) pull their data from Apple, so once you've submitted to this directory, a lot of other directories (such as Podcast Addict, Pocket Casts and Overcast) will list it too.

Type: Short Task

Time Required: 5 minutes to submit, up to 7 working days to be approved and listed

Podcast Level: From the beginning

How to Do It

Find your RSS feed link inside your hosting provider dashboard. Log in to podcastsconnect.apple.com (you will need to create an Apple account if you don't already have one). Click on the + symbol, and copy in your RSS feed. Check/edit the show details and hit submit. It can take anywhere from 24 hours to 7 working days to hear from Apple (this can be even longer during holiday periods). Apple will email you to tell you whether or not your show has been accepted. The most common reasons for rejection are incorrect cover art specs, or podcast names they believe are "keyword stuffing". For more guidance on this, check out the links in the Further Reading section.

Task List:

☐ If you don't already have an Apple login, create one.

☐ Log Into Apple Podcasts (iTunes) Connect.

☐ Click the blue + symbol to add a new RSS feed.

☐ Copy-paste your RSS feed URL (or type it in, if you like) into the box where they ask for it.

□ Apple Podcasts Connect will display your podcasts in the window, with the status, "Submitted for review."

Further Reading:

- The Top Podcast Directories to Widen Your Podcast Distribution

  > thepodcasthost.com/directories

- How to Get Your Podcast On iTunes/Apple Podcasts

  > thepodcasthost.com/applepodcasts

- Podcast Names: What Should I Call My Podcast?

  > thepodcasthost.com/podcastnames

- How to Create Great Podcast Cover Art

  > thepodcasthost.com/coverart

2. Spotify

Spotify has put a lot of work into battling Apple for King Of The Mountain when it comes to market share. Spotify is a popular choice for Android phones and mobile devices. Their listening app tends to imitate top-40 radio, emphasizing big-label short pop songs punctuated with advertising. It's not created with podcasts in mind. However, recently, they've become interested in podcasters and their data, so the Spotify for Podcasters dashboard can be helpful.

Type: Short Task

Time Required: 5 minutes to submit, 1-2 working days to be approved and listed

Podcast Level: From the beginning

How to Do It

There are two ways to get your podcast on Spotify. One is to do it through your media host, and the other is to submit it through the Spotify For Podcasters portal. Even if you submit it through your media host, you should still claim it, so you can use the Spotify Dashboard.

The Spotify For Podcasters dashboard lets you see how your podcast is doing within Spotify. It shows you the number of starts, streams, and listeners. It also shows you at what point in the episode people stopped listening. This provides a useful sample when it comes to reviewing your content.

Caveat emptor: whether your podcast has ads or not, Spotify listeners will hear ads in between your podcast episodes, unless they pay for Spotify's subscription service.

Task List:

☐ Through your media host: follow the instructions provided by your media host.

- ☐ Through Spotify for Podcasters:

- ☐ Create a login and sign in.

- ☐ Click on "Claim your podcast" or "Submit Your Podcast"

- ☐ Read the terms and click agree

- ☐ Give them your RSS feed.

- ☐ Claim your podcast.

Further Reading:

- How to Get Your Podcast On Spotify

  > thepodcasthost.com/getonspotify

3. Google Podcasts

Google has had a funny relationship with podcasts over the years. The search giants have dipped their toe in the water several times, often resulting in half-baked schemes like having some podcasts available on Google Play Music. However, Google Podcasts finally seems to be a serious effort by the company to fully embrace podcasting.

Type: Short Task

Time Required: 5 minutes to check if your show is already there (it probably is)

Podcast Level: From the beginning

How to Do It

Google Podcasts bucks the RSS feed submission process by taking a "don't call us, we'll call you" approach. If your podcast is already in places like Apple Podcasts and Spotify, you're probably already available in Google Podcasts, too.

However, they do now have an interface - podcastmanager.google.com - where you can essentially manage your show inside Google Podcasts. By default, this can act as a submission prompt for Google if your show isn't already listed with them.

Task List:

☐ If you don't already have a Google account, set one up.

☐ Go to Google Podcasts Manager.

☐ Click on "Start Now."

☐ Enter your podcast's RSS feed.

☐ Preview how your podcast looks on Google, to make sure everything is correct.

☐ The final step is to verify ownership. If the RSS feed email and the email you used to log into Google Podcast Manager don't match, Google sends an email to verify that you own the RSS feed.

☐ Otherwise, if the email addresses are the same, Google says that no verification is needed. Click the submit button.

Further Reading:

- Google Podcasts Manager: How to Submit or Claim Your Show

  > thepodcasthost.com/googlepodcastmanager

4. Stitcher

Stitcher was *the* Android podcast listening app, and *the* directory for celebrity podcasts and paid subscriptions, before other app developers tried to make a "Netflix For Podcasts." Its reputation now is that it tends to be buggy, and has problematic user reviews (according to The Verge.com). Nevertheless, it has a loyal following, and you should at least submit your podcast to them. Stitcher says that you can use Amazon's Alexa and Echo devices to play any podcast that's available on Stitcher.

Type: Short Task

Time Required: 5 minutes to submit, 2-4 working days to be approved and listed

Podcast Level: From the beginning

How to Do It

By this point, you have probably figured out that these processes are mostly the same. In the case of Stitcher, they offer download information via their Provider Portal, they "don't strip out your ads," and they are working on monetization partnership schemes. It's worth your time to read Stitcher's FAQ, just as you would any directory.

Task List:

☐ Go to the Stitcher Partner Portal.

☐ Submit your RSS feed & create a login.

☐ Stitcher sends a message to the email address associated with your RSS feed (the one you used when you set up your media hosting account). This is for your security. Click on the link provided in the email.

☐ Once you've done this, Stitcher approves your podcast's inclusion within 24 hours.

Further Reading:

- Stitcher + Podcast Creators portal

  > thepodcasthost.com/stitcherportal

5. TuneIn

TuneIn is an odd duck. Their submission process looks like a website contact form, and it's buried in their FAQ. They also say that any changes you need to make to your podcast (such as updating your cover art), you need to do via a separate contact form, also buried in their FAQ (but your RSS feed would do this anyway). However, it has a following, it has loyal users, and there's no reason not to submit your podcast to them. Apparently if you have submitted your podcast to TuneIn, and it shows up in a directory search, then it's on Amazon. But, if you listen to a podcast on Alexa through TuneIn, you can't stop and start where you left off.

Type: Short Task

Time Required: 15 minutes

Podcast Level: From the beginning

How to Do It

You will need your RSS feed and some of the information from your media host. The process is pretty much the same as any other directory.

Task List:

☐ Fill out this email form, which can be found deep within TuneIn's FAQ: thepodcasthost.com/tuneinsubmission

☐ Send it to TuneIn.

☐ Verify that the email address associated with the RSS feed is correct.

Further Reading:

• TuneIn for Podcasters

> thepodcasthost.com/tuneinforpodcasters

- TuneIn Submission

  > thepodcasthost.com/tuneinsubmission

6. Amazon Alexa/Echo

Many people tell their smart speaker to play their favourite podcast for them, when they can't be bothered to find a podcast in a directory or on an app, or they have their hands in a sink full of soapsuds.

Type: Short Task

Time Required: 15 minutes

Podcast Level: From the beginning

How To Do It

Some media hosts (Libsyn, for example) will create a dedicated Alexa 'Skill' for you. But your show will be available through these devices already if you've submitted to directories like TuneIn or Stitcher.

With smart speakers, consider that not everything is spelled the way it sounds. It might be easy for Alexa to understand that you want to hear, "Hostile Worlds" but it might not understand a title like, "Jarnsaxa Rising." If you're still in the early stages of planning your podcast, you may want to think about spelling and pronunciation when selecting a title.

This is another reason why trying to keyword-stuff your show title is a bad idea. By the time the voice in the tube has informed you that it is "now playing Podcraft - the podcast for podcasters who want to learn how to start a podcast, buy a microphone, sign up to a hosting provider, launch their show, grow their audience, and earn money from their content", your washing up will be finished.

Task List:

☐ Submit your show to Stitcher and TuneIn.

☐ Test out finding and playing your show on your smart speaker, via these platforms.

☐ If you host with Libsyn, contact them to get a dedicated Alexa Skill made .

Further Reading:

- How to Get an Amazon Alexa Skill for Your Podcast

  > thepodcasthost.com/alexa

7. Radio Public

Radio Public is a really pretty, interesting podcast directory. They organize their selections by unusual criteria, including audience mood. Listeners have an option to tip podcasters. This directory also works really hard to ensure producer loyalty, by offering marketing courses and other options (such as a "free 21-day marketing course").

Type: Short Task

Time Required: 15 minutes

Podcast Level: From the beginning

How To Do It

Again, have your RSS feed and other information ready, and be ready to verify ownership. It's pretty straightforward. They will ask if you want to buy a RadioPublic pro account, which is optional. RadioPublic also lets you pick "gateway episodes" to display on the Radio Public page. This is especially good if you have trailer episodes or standalone episodes to tempt new listeners.

Task List:

☐ Visit Radiopublic's podcaster portal: thepodcasthost.com/radiopublic.

☐ Click "Get Started." A popup window will ask you to verify ownership of your podcast.

☐ Enter the RSS feed address.

☐ You will get an email at the address associated with the RSS feed.

☐ Verify that you own the podcast.

Further Reading:

- RadioPublic's Podcaster Portal

  > thepodcasthost.com/radiopublic

8. Podchaser

If you have submitted your podcast to Apple, and it's accepted, your podcast is on Podchaser. You'll want to "claim" it on there, though, because it gives you some good ways to promote your podcast.

For example, if your interview show has a guest who's been on other shows, or if you swap interviews with other hosts, you can add your shows to those networks. You can make lists of podcasts with common traits, and share those lists. There is a guest database to find guests for your show, or to be a guest on someone else's. Users can leave reviews. Podchaser has a strong social media element, that is great for people who truly love podcasts.

Podchaser is working to integrate with other media companies that do interesting things in the podcast world (such as *Headliner*), so it's worth it to keep an eye on what they're doing.

Type: Short Task

Time Required: 10 minutes

Podcast Level: From the beginning

How To Do It

Like social media, you create a login and profile, then claim your podcast. Once you've done this, surf around and check out the features. Podchaser really is more like a combination of Facebook and IMDb for podcasts.

What if your podcast isn't on Podchaser? Go to Podchaser's FAQ. Find the question about "how to submit a podcast." A popup window appears. Enter the RSS feed address in the box, and submit it. Podchaser doesn't include RSS feeds which aren't publicly available. So, if a podcast is private (such as a subscriber-only podcast or an intra-company podcast), it won't be on Podchaser.

Task List:

☐ Create a login.

☐ Fill out your profile.

☐ Make sure it looks like how you'd want it to look on any social media outlet.

☐ Search for your podcast and click the button to claim it.

☐ Podchaser gives you a form to fill out.

☐ They send an email to the address associated with the podcast's RSS feed, with a numeric code.

☐ Enter the code on your podcast's page to claim it.

Further Reading:

• Using Podchaser to Grow Your Audience

> thepodcasthost.com/podchasergrowth

Online Communities

"People rarely succeed unless they have fun in what they are doing."- Dale Carnegie

C ommunities make the world go 'round, as far as the Internet is concerned. They're a place where conversations happen, word of mouth is spread, and the relationships can incite folks to move out and explore other areas (such as your podcast, its website, events, merchandise, and so on). In this section, we'll talk about some ways you can use online communities to best advantage.

1. **Start an Online Community**

2. **Contribute Constructively to Another Community**

3. **Find the Right Communities**

1. Start an Online Community

Creating an online community about your podcast and its topic lets you engage in discussion with your podcast audience. It allows you to get feedback, and generate enthusiasm.

Type: Regular Technique

Time Required: Take an hour to set it up, and then use it for an hour or two on a regular basis (weekly, for example). Consistency is key.

Podcast Level: From the beginning

How to Do It

One option is to create a community through your Wordpress site. Creating a community on your own site is great, because you have more control. However, it's a bit more work. You can also build community within existing social media platforms. In this case, you relinquish control over the community's discussion space, but you can concentrate more on discussion content. This also means that you're subject to the whims of the platform you choose.

If you want to create a community on your own Wordpress site, then you'll want to use a plugin. Here are a couple.

bbPress

bbPress is focused on ease of integration, ease of use, web standards, and speed. You can basically build this plugin into any type of forum you like while still allowing for great add-on features through WordPress's extensive plugin system.

CM Answers

This plugin is more basic. It's not a full forum package but a question and answer type of forum. People can post a question, anyone can post an answer, and you can get the voting up answers type of functionality, that you find in Stackoverflow, Yahoo Answers and so on.

Alternative Options

If you choose to use a social media platform, then find a platform you like, read their rules, and set it up.

Facebook Groups is a good option for online discussion and sharing of posts. People can share on their own schedule, and discuss at their own pace. However, some people dislike it, because Facebook groups can be a target for misinformation, or just plain rude behaviour. Since people can post and comment in your group at any time, the discussion might need moderation at any time. You don't want your fly-fishing podcast group to be tainted by someone smearing a political candidate, or trying to sell fake designer sunglasses. Read Facebook's privacy policies with regard to groups for details.

Another option is to use a chat system, such as Discord. Discord is a highly customizable voice communication and chat tool, originally designed for gamers. It's meant to be fun. This would let your audience chat with you and each other. Plus, you're there to answer questions or be aware of any problems that arise. Make a consistent, regular appointment for discussion. You can call it something novel & related to your podcast, like "Hostile Worlds' Landing Bay" or "Organic Life's Farm Stand." Having a meeting in a finite time window encourages people to think about the questions they want to ask beforehand, and to use the time mindfully, rather than just posting impulsively in an online group. You will have to remind your audience about the online community meetings. Include it in your CTA.

Zoom is a great option for online community meetings if you want to share visual content. The free version of Zoom lets you have up to ten people in a meeting, which can last forty minutes.

Instagram is a social media system where people share photos and videos. You can set up an account that's tied to your podcast, and then use it to share photos, visual art, and images of text. You can also use it to share video and audiograms.

Task list:

☐ Check out BBPress and CMAnswers.

☐ Start building a basic forum, using the plugin's instructions.

☐ Build a few different sections for that forum based on your topic. Center one section around general guidelines and announcements.

☐ Invite your audience to join the forum, in your episodes' call to action, show notes, and social media posts.

☐ Start discussions in the topic threads with questions related to your podcast topic.

☐ Check in to make sure people are using the forum constructively.

☐ Take a look at Facebook Groups, Discord, Instagram, and Zoom. Decide which is best for you.

☐ Set up your Facebook Group, Discord, or other discussion group according to their instructions.

☐ Include your online community in your Call To Action. Emphasize how much you'd like to "meet" your listeners there.

☐ In your online community, include content inspired by your podcast episodes, but with different media, such as pictures, memes, video, polls, and Q&As.

Related to: Enabling Your Existing Audience, Helping Others To Help Yourself, Gaining New Visibility, Organic Social Media

Further Reading:

• Information about the bbpress plugin on Wordpress.org.

   > thepodcasthost.com/bbpress

• Information about the CMAnswers plugin on Wordpress.org.

> thepodcasthost.com/cmanswers

- Creating a 'Real Life' Podcast Community

  > thepodcasthost.com/reallifecommunity

- Building a Community

  > thepodcasthost.com/buildingcommunity

- Digital Sharecropping: The Most Dangerous Threat to Your Content Marketing Strategy, by Copyblogger

  > thepodcasthost.com/digitalsharecropping

2. Contribute Constructively to Another Community

Joining an online community dedicated to your topic of interest is a great way to grow your show, provided you let others in the community lead. Listening and contributing in a way that adds genuine value builds trust. This can make people more interested in what you have to offer. It's true that you can lead a horse to water, but you can't make it drink. However, if you put clean water in an area where there are horses, they will eventually come over and drink on their own.

Type: Regular Technique

Time Required: 15 minutes at a time, up to an hour a week

Podcast Level: From the beginning

How to Do It

This is where your love of your podcast's topic will take the wheel. Let's say you have a podcast about thrift (charity) shops. So you join a group on Facebook dedicated to unusual thrift shops. People post pictures and talk about great shops they've found, unusual things they've seen or bought in thrift shops, and so on. If you come in on day one saying "Hello everyone, I have a podcast about thrift shops and you all should listen to it," you'll just alienate people. What you owe it to yourself to do is read, watch, and see what the content and dynamic of the group are. How compatible are their discussions with your podcast? What are the big concerns? Are they talking about Goodwill vs. Salvation Army, or the prevalence of costume jewellery? You might find shop owners to interview, or topics to discuss on your podcast. When you feel comfortable, and you've added some value to the group, then mention that you have a podcast.

Task List:

☐ Find a few online communities related to your podcast's topic.

☐ Join them, follow the group guidelines, read and watch the group for a few weeks.

☐ Let yourself be inspired by what's happening in the group.

☐ If there are discussions where you can honestly add value (i.e., "I know a great way to get stains out of velvet!"), then participate.

☐ Use your knowledge and expertise with compassion.

Related to: Helping Others To Help Yourself, Organic Social Media

Further Reading:

• Creating a 'Real Life' Podcast Community

    > thepodcasthost.com/reallifecommunity

• Building a Community

    > thepodcasthost.com/buildingcommunity

3. Find the Right Communities

Not all communities will be a good fit to grow your podcast. On the other hand, some will be a great fit. If they help you grow your show, terrific. If not, put your time and energy into something else.

Type: Short Task

Time Required: Less than an hour

Podcast Level: From the beginning

How to Do It

Ask other podcasters with shows like yours if they'd recommend any communities, or do a Google search for related communities.

Check the rules and regulations on the community, as well as the platform.

As you're looking at a community, ask yourself some questions before posting or fully participating in the discussion. How do you feel about its values? What kind of language do people use? Is it generally uplifting? Do people share information constructively, or are there petty arguments? Do members feel comfortable sharing photos or links to outside information? Are there meetups?

If reading through the discussion doesn't make you feel good, give it a pass. If it does, listen and learn.

Task List:

☐ Search on Google for online communities related to your podcast topic.

☐ Ask other podcasters with shows like yours if they'd recommend any communities.

☐ When you find a community, read the rules and regulations.

☐ Read some of the discussions. Check with your gut instincts.

Related to: other techniques/strategies that work well with this.

Further Reading:

- Creating a 'Real Life' Podcast Community

    > thepodcasthost.com/reallifecommunity

- Building a Community

    > thepodcasthost.com/buildingcommunity

Helping Yourself By Helping Others

"A rising tide lifts all boats" - Sean Lemass

With things like promotion and growth, we can be fooled into thinking that we need to channel all our energy into talking about our own stuff. But, often the opposite is true.

The internet's a noisy place, and people tend to tune obvious self-promotion out. But through helping promote others, you can also raise your own profile, build relationships, and get in front of lots more people.

That's the purpose of this chapter. Here, you'll learn some tips and strategies that'll help you to promote and grow the audience *of others*. In turn, this will lead to more interest (and ultimately, more ears) on your own content!

1. **Tweet About Another Podcast**

2. **Run a Co-Hosted Episode**

3. **Create a Montage Episode**

4. **Create a 'Best Podcasts For...' Roundup**

5. **Review a Product or Service**

6. **Create a Sponsored Resource**

7. **Support a Charity**

8. **Write a Guest Post**

9. **Help Crowdfund Another Podcast**

1. Tweet About Another Podcast

The most obvious way to promote your podcast on Twitter, is to tweet about your own show. But could you actually see better results by tweeting about someone else's stuff?

There's probably other podcasts out there in your niche that helped inspire you towards creating your own. If they share your target audience, then tweeting about them might get you some visibility in front of their listeners.

On top of that, it can also help you to build relationships and grow your network.

Type: Short Task

Time Required: Less than 5 minutes

Podcast Level: From episode 1

How to Do It

Pick an established show that you like, one that's pretty active on twitter and has a decent sized following.

Tag them in a tweet, and thank them for being one of the inspirations behind starting your own podcast. Or, you can say what you enjoy about the podcast. You can mention the name of your show, or maybe you'll be tweeting directly from a dedicated podcast account.

In any case, a reply, like, or retweet from them will have your tweet show up in the feeds of their followers. Some of them will inevitably be curious, and check out your podcast.

Task List:

☐ (Optional) set up a dedicated twitter account for your podcast.

☐ Pick an established show you like, in a similar niche as you.

☐ Tag them in a tweet thanking them for being an inspiration behind your show.

☐ Be sure to have a link to your podcast website in your bio.

2. Run a Co-Hosted Episode

Teaming up with another podcast in your niche to do a special co-hosted episode can be a great way to expand your reach.

You both have your own audiences, but combining forces to create content for them can have an "audience share" effect.

These "crossover" episodes can bring fresh and engaging content to the listeners of both shows.

They can also help listeners find new, relevant, and enjoyable content that they might not have already been aware of.

Type: Big Strategy

Time Required: The usual amount of time it takes you to complete an episode, plus a few extra days for communication.

Podcast Level: At least 20 episodes.

How to Do It

The first step is to find another podcast that's at a similar level to your own show, in terms of influence and following.

This podcast should also be similar in topic to your own, or have some sort of overlap in subject matter.

Once you find a show that looks like a good fit, reach out to them and propose a special co-hosted episode on a topic that'll benefit both your audiences.

Be sure to sell the benefits to them. You think your audience will love their content, and this is an opportunity to grow their reach.

Publish this special episode on both your feeds, making it clear throughout that this is a co-hosted episode between podcast X and podcast Y.

Task List:

☐ Identify the podcast you'd like to collaborate with.

☐ Come up with a useful and interesting episode topic.

☐ Reach out to them with your proposal.

☐ Sell the benefits to them - this can help grow their reach!

☐ Plan and record your episode.

☐ Publish it on both podcast feeds.

Related to: Create a Montage Episode

3. Create a Montage Episode

A montage episode is a piece of audio content, made up of clips from different contributors.

A tried and tested way of creating one is to build the episode around a single topic or question. Each participant records their answer to the question, and sends over their audio to the creator.

You can collect clips from anyone from the general public, to your podcast listeners. In this particular instance, we want to create one with fellow podcasters in our niche.

Type: Big Strategy

Time Required: Around 3 months, from planning to publishing

Podcast Level: About 10 episodes, or at the end of a season

How to Do It

Firstly, you need to decide on a topic for your episode. Choose something that's going to be interesting and useful to the audiences of all involved.

Some examples of montage episodes could include

- An episode of a travel podcast, where contributors talk about their favourite holiday destination

- An episode of a sound design podcast, where contributors talk about their favourite audio production software

- An episode of a health podcast, where contributors talk about their morning routines

You may be asking a single question, but it's a good idea to have some prompts alongside it.

Imagine the hypothetical travel podcast creates a montage episode titled "The World's Best Holiday Destinations", and one of the clips is someone simply saying "Jamaica". That would be a pretty dull and pointless episode.

When asking for contributions, you might expand on the question "what is your favourite holiday destination?" with any of the following;

- Why did you choose to go there?

- What's your favourite memory of the place?

- What's something that surprised you about it?

- What's your top tip for someone planning to go there in the future?

This will help give yourself the best possible chance of gathering great, insightful content.

Decide too, if you'd like to put an approximate time guide on answers. Between 3-5 minutes is always a good sweet spot. But don't be too strict with this, or you'll discourage folks from participating.

You'll want to set a deadline for getting the clips back, so you can begin production. Lay out specific instructions in an easy-to-skim manner. These are things like

- When you need the clip sent over by

- Where or how to send it

- Any file format or naming preferences

Once you have the clips together, assemble them in a good running order. You can then script your own parts in the episode - the intro and outro, as well as any commentary you'd like to add in between clips.

When you've published a montage episode, be sure to reach out to everyone involved and ask them to share it with their own listeners. Everyone's podcast can grow with this strategy, on top of it being great content for the collective audience. Everyone wins!

Task List:

- ☐ Identify the podcasts you'd like to collaborate with.

- ☐ Come up with a useful and interesting episode topic.

- ☐ Reach out to them with your proposal.

- ☐ Sell the benefits to them - this can help grow their reach!

- ☐ Lay out your specific instructions.

- ☐ Gather in audio clips.

- ☐ Record and intro and outro, and any commentary.

- ☐ Mix episode together.

- ☐ Publish.

- ☐ Share with all involved - ask them to share it too.

Related to: Co-hosted episodes

Further Reading:

- Growing Your Audience With a Milestone Episode

  > thepodcasthost.com/montage

4. Create a 'Best Podcasts For...' Roundup

Lists, or 'roundups', are one of the most shareable (and searchable) forms of content on the planet.

The concept is simple. A roundup is a piece of content with a list of the author's favourite, or top recommended things, built around a particular question or topic.

A great way to utilise them to grow your audience, is to create a 'Best Podcasts for...' roundup in your niche. This could either be done as a podcast episode, or blog post (or both!).

An example of us using this tactic would be in our 'Best Space Podcasts' roundup, which we used to help promote our space podcast Hostile Worlds. You can see it at thepodcasthost.com/spacepodcasts

Type: Short Task

Time Required: 3 hours

Podcast Level: From episode 1

How to Do It

Compile a list of podcasts - say, 5 to 7 - and build an episode or article with them using the "Best Podcasts for..." or "Best ___ Podcasts" title structure.

Talk a bit about each one. What's it about? Who's it by? Why do you like it? How has it been useful to you? Why do you recommend others go and check it out? Be sure to provide links to each show's website too.

In your intro or summary to this roundup, mention that you also run a podcast in this niche and that these shows have helped and inspired you. Here, you can link back to your own show, and even play a promo trailer for it.

When you've published your roundup, email and tweet each of the podcasts mentioned. Tell them about their inclusion on the list, and ask them if they wouldn't mind sharing it with their audience too.

This doesn't actually need to be a "best podcasts" roundup either. It could just as easily be a roundup of websites, businesses, services – anything that's going to be helpful to your audience!

Task List:

☐ Decide on your title.

☐ Draft the list of podcasts you'd like to include.

☐ Record and/or write your roundup.

☐ Be sure to mention and link back to your own show.

☐ Publish.

☐ Share with everyone mentioned - email them, tag them on social.

☐ Ask them to share it with their own audience.

Related to: Review a Product or Service

5. Review a Product or Service

You can create shareable content that'll help grow your audience by reviewing a product or service.

For example, if you do a cooking podcast, and use a certain type of whisk, you could review it on an episode, then get in touch with the company who makes it and let them know. The chances are, they'll share it with their own audience, many of whom will be interested in your podcast.

A couple of other examples could be

- a biking show that reviews a pair of cycling shoes

- a podcasting show that reviews a microphone or mixer

The idea is to do a podcast episode, video, or blog post reviewing something relevant and helpful to your audience. Something in your niche that you yourself use and endorse.

Type: Short Task

Time Required: 3 hours

Podcast Level: 10 episodes or more

How to Do It

Pick a product or service relevant to your topic, that you use and endorse. Something that'll be useful and interesting to your audience.

Write or record a review of it. Who are the folks behind it? Why did you start using it? How much does it cost? What problem or issue was it designed to solve? What results have you had with it? It's always more engaging and authentic if you can build in personal stories and real life examples here.

Once you've published your review, reach out to the company behind the product or service. They'll likely want to share it out with their own audience and customer base.

There might also be the opportunity to strike up a partnership deal through affiliate or sponsorship. The company might even send you more stuff to review.

If it's a purely written review, remember to make it clear in your article that you run a podcast. Embed a player in there of your promo trailer, and include a link to your subscribe page too!

Task List:

- ☐ Choose a relevant product or service to review.

- ☐ Write or record your review - preferably both!

- ☐ Be sure to include links to your podcast in the article.

- ☐ Reach out to company behind product or service.

- ☐ Ask them to share your review on their social or email list.

- ☐ Enquire about possible future sponsorship, affiliate, or partnership possibilities.

Related to: Create a Sponsored Resource

6. Create a Sponsored Resource

When a business sponsors a podcast, we traditionally think of money changing hands. But sponsorships can also work as content partnerships, where the podcaster is paid in visibility and potential new listeners, rather than cash.

These arrangements can be easier to set up, and far more rewarding in the long term than being paid a small one-off fee.

A sponsored resource is basically something you can create for a business. It should be something that their customers will find useful, or enjoy. In exchange, the resource - and the business itself - will promote your podcast and send new listeners your way.

So, what could a few examples of this look like? As ever with podcasting, it'll totally depend on your topic, but how about;

- An outdoors podcast who create a PDF resource for a popular walking boot company - "The Top 20 Walking Trails in Scotland"

- A ketogenic diet podcast who create a PDF resource or infographic, for a cheese or butter company, with 20 exciting recipes to try.

Type: Big Strategy

Time Required: Multiple weeks, or potentially months from initial outreach, to discussion, to resource creation.

Podcast Level: At least 25 episodes

How to Do It

Firstly, you should identify the company you'd love to partner with. This should be a company whose products or services you use and endorse.

Reach out to their marketing department, and ask to speak to someone with regards to advertising opportunities. Lay out some ideas for them of the resource you'd like to create. If you can create a 'prototype' version of your resource to show them how it all looks, that might help capture their interest.

For this, it's also a good idea to have a media kit, so they can get a bit of background to what the show is about, and why it exists.

Agree on the terms of your relationship, and establish your roles. Your role might be simply to create the content. It should naturally be content that their customers and audience will enjoy.

Their role might then be to share the resource on their social media channels. This encourages folks to use their product, and it also advertises your own podcast. It's a win-win.

Task List:

☐ Choose a product or service you use and endorse.

☐ Reach out to their marketing department.

☐ Propose your resource idea (create and show them a 'prototype', if possible)

☐ Explain why it's useful for them.

☐ Explain what you're looking for in return.

☐ **Related to:** Review a Product or Service

Further Reading:

• How to Make a Podcast Media Kit

> thepodcasthost.com/mediakit

7. Support a Charity

Getting behind a charity that's close to your heart - as well as your podcast topic - can build a great win-win scenario for all involved.

Such support could be financial, but it may be more useful to both parties for you to promote and spotlight the work of the organisation.

If you do an interview show, partnering with a charity may give you access to folks who'd love to do an episode with you.

If you're creating good content around a charity, they'll likely want to share and promote your podcast to their wider audience.

Again, it all depends on your topic, but a couple of examples could be;

- A tabletop wargaming podcast supporting a veterans charity.

- Or a writers' show supporting an organisation that helps fund books for kids in socially deprived neighbourhoods.

Obviously, with charities, it'll be more of a long term reciprocity thing, rather than a direct transaction of whatever you can offer, in exchange for promotion. You'll need to be respectful here, and be aware that this is an ongoing relationship, rather than a service.

Type: Big Strategy

Time Required: Multiple weeks, or potentially months from initial outreach, to discussion, to resource creation.

Podcast Level: 10 episodes or more

How to Do It

It starts with identifying a charity that's both close to your heart, and close to your topic.

Every organised charity will have a team or a person who's responsible for its growth. This will essentially be a marketing department, though it might be called something else. With many charities, this role is carried out by a single person.

It's good to reach out with some solid proposals of how you'd like to work together. But also asking the question of, "how could I help you?" is going to be useful.

With most things in life, especially charities, one big answer to this will be "money". You may not be in a position to directly donate money, but you could incorporate this into your episode CTAs as opposed to asking for personal support on platforms like Patreon.

It doesn't necessarily need to be around money though. Any charity is going to appreciate positive media coverage, and being offered a platform to share their news, updates, and opinions.

So explain to them the things you could offer on that front. This could be anything from regular interviews, to an ongoing 2 minute "spotlight" section at the end of each episode with news and updates.

The key is that you're still creating interesting and useful content for your podcast too. So make sure you never agree to anything that sacrifices that.

If they do initially ask you if you'd be looking for anything in return, you might enquire about a mention for your podcast on their social media, website, or newsletter.

Task List:

☐ Choose a charity close to your topic (and heart)

☐ Reach out to the person or department responsible for their marketing.

☐ Propose some ways your podcast can help them.

☐ Also, ask them what they most need help with.

☐ Agree to run a trial period of 4-6 episodes and see how it works out for both parties.

8. Write a Guest Post

A popular way to promote your podcast is to do a guest post on a site with a similar target audience. With a guest post, you're creating insightful and helpful content for their readers, and in turn, are able to link back to your own content.

Type: Big Strategy

Time Required: 2-6 week turnaround

Podcast Level: 10 episodes or more

How to Do It

Firstly, you need to identify the website you'd like to write your guest post for. This should be a site with the same, or similar target audience as yourself.

Some websites have guidelines for guest submissions, which make the process a lot easier. If the site you've picked out doesn't have any mention of guest posting though, then you'll need to reach out to them directly with a proposal.

Ultimately, what the website owner will want to hear, is;

- What you would like to write about

- Why it would be useful and interesting to their audience

- Credibility - a little about you, and why you're well positioned to help

- The benefits their audience will get from it

- What keywords or search terms you are targeting

- The ways you will share the post to drive traffic to their site

- What you would like in return (simply, to mention your podcast in the article summary)

At The Podcast Host we try to do guest posts on a regular basis. We've done a few for podcast equipment and sound effect companies, as well as sites that focus more on writing and content creation.

It can be useful to pitch something that brings your own unique perspective to the table, and not just something the site owner could easily write themselves. For example, at the time of writing, we are in the process of doing a guest post for microphone giants RODE. Our article will be titled "5 ways to improve your podcast that don't involve tech".

RODE like this idea because they are a tech company, and they can easily demonstrate how good their gear is. But once their audience buys their stuff, they'll want to go and create content with it. That's why this article could be really helpful to them, and they'll be grateful to RODE for publishing it!

Task List:

- [ ] Pick out a few websites you'd love to publish guest posts on.

- [ ] Check if they have guest post guidelines (if so, follow them!)

- [ ] Reach out to them with your proposal.

- [ ] Sell the benefits. Why will this be great for them, and their audience?

- [ ] Ask for permission to mention your podcast (and link back to it) in the article summary. Or in your author bio.

Related to: Be Interviewed on Another Podcast

9. Help Crowdfund Another Podcast

If there's one thing 99% of podcasts have in common, it's in asking their listeners for financial support.

Commonly, this is done through crowdfunding platforms like Patreon. And in exchange for supporting them, many shows will offer reward tiers that can help promote the work of the patron.

If you have some disposable cash to spare, there are worse ways to spend it. You're helping to support a fellow creative, and have the opportunity to grow your own show in exchange.

Type: Ongoing Strategy

Time Required: 5mins to set up

Podcast Level: At any point

How to Do It

There's an increasing number of crowdfunding sites on the web these days. They're split into two main types;

1. The one-off. Where supporters donate to work towards one big goal, in order to fund something new. Think Kickstarter, or Indiegogo.

2. The ongoing. Where supporters donate a fee per month, or per creation. Think Patreon, or Buy Me A Coffee.

If there are podcasts out there that you like, with a similar target audience, listen out to see if they're asking for support on any of these platforms. Then, check out if they're offering any rewards.

These rewards could be things like;

1. Putting a link to your website on their own site

2. Mentioning you on their show

3. Playing your trailer on their show

Sign up based on what reward you'd like best, along with what you can comfortably afford. If you love the idea of doing this, but are strapped for cash, consider setting up your own crowdfunding venture, then use the money you earn to pass on directly to other creators.

Task List:

☐ Pick out some potential podcasts in your niche that you'd like to support.

☐ Find out if they run any crowdfunding.

☐ See what rewards they offer, and pledge to one you like (and can afford)

☐ If you're short on money, start your own crowdfunding venture!

Related to: Advertising Your Podcast

Further Reading:

• Patreon for Podcasters: Best Practices

> thepodcasthost.com/patreon

Attending Live Events

"Courage starts with showing up and letting ourselves be seen." - Brene Brown

Attending live events (such as conventions, conferences, and meetups) can help you in many ways. You can enhance word of mouth about your podcast, meet experts on your show's topics, learn more about the topic's challenges, and develop strategies for overcoming them. It'll give you food for thought for future episode planning, as well as spreading the word. In this chapter, you'll learn about:

1. **Meetup.com**

2. **Finding Conferences in Your Niche**

3. **Partnering With an Event**

4. **Vox-Pops**

5. **Smaller Clubs and Societies**

1. Meetup.com

Meetup.com describes their business as "a platform for finding and building local communities. People use Meetup to meet new people, learn new things, find support, get out of their comfort zones, and pursue their passions, together." Essentially, you can search by interest and location to find events where you can meet other people interested in your podcast's topic.

Face to face interaction goes a long way toward promoting your podcast. Other people are more likely to remember you (and your work), if they have met you in person.

It's a lower-risk proposition to attend a local, smaller event. You can also look at websites like meetup.com or Eventbrite, to find groups in your area. Facebook has some niche groups which host live events.

These tend to be held at pubs, libraries, or coffee shops. They're a chance to socialize and learn from each other.

Type: Big Strategy

Time Required: A few minutes to search, more time to attend local events

Podcast Level: After at least 5-10 episodes

How To Do It

Go to Meetup.com and sign up for an account. There are many categories of interests you can look through, or you can search by keyword. You can adapt the geographic search radius to find where these events are held. These events tend to be on the smaller, more local side, so it can be a good place to try out networking, before you start going to bigger events.

Bring cash in small bills with you. Coffee shops or pubs that host these sorts of events do so with the expectation that people will buy food and/or drink. Other spaces might pass a collection basket to pay for the cost of renting the meeting space. If you're meeting at an event that serves alcohol, don't depend on it for confidence.

Task List:

- ☐ Go to Meetup.com and Eventbrite, and sign up for an account.

- ☐ On Meetup, create a profile, listing interests which are relevant to your podcast topic.

- ☐ Find and sign up to relevant groups.

- ☐ Search on these websites to find local meetings you can attend.

- ☐ Go to a meeting. Be polite and listen. Keep an open mind.

- ☐ When you get home, take a moment to write some notes about what you learned and who you met.

- ☐ Decide if you'd like to attend again. You should try at least three.

Related to: Online Communities, Organic Social Media, Helping Others To Help Yourself

Further Reading:

- Creating a 'Real Life' Podcast Community

  > thepodcasthost.com/reallifecommunity

2. Finding Conferences In Your Niche

It's worth your time to get on the mailing list for the big conventions and conferences related to your topic. Often, these mailing lists will promote smaller local events, and share informative articles. Businesses sometimes sponsor these, so it can be a good way to get to know brands associated with your content.

Attending one of the bigger events requires more commitment, but potentially greater reward. Depending on the event, and where you live, you have to pay for travel, accommodation, food, and the entry admission. This can run into hundreds, if not thousands of dollars. Subscribing to the event mailing list should help you get some discount codes.

The good news is that you can get to meet people from a greater distance away from home, and learn from people you might not otherwise. Also, people who enjoy your podcast get to meet you.

Type: Big Strategy

Time Required: A week to a month, depending on the conference

Podcast Level: At least 10 episodes

How to Do It

Politeness always counts. You don't want to come swaggering in bragging about your podcast from the get-go. Keep your mind open, be observant, and ready to learn.

Take note of the panel discussions, lectures and workshops available. What can you learn from them? Are there activities you're most interested in? Sometimes, asking a question at a Q&A is a way to name-drop your podcast, while a microphone is in front of you and folks are listening.

Bring a bottle of water, stay hydrated, and get plenty of rest when you're not learning or networking. Wear comfortable shoes and plan to be moving around quite a bit.

Bring business cards for your podcast, with a QR code on the back, linking to your podcast website. Don't feel that you have to jettison them constantly like a blackjack dealer. If you have a good conversation with someone, the moment feels right, and you want to link them to your podcast, give them a business card. Similarly, stickers are popular. If you can get a lot of them, inexpensively, to give out, it's likely that people will put them on their laptop or water bottle where they can be seen by others.

If you're experienced with conventions, conferences and big events, your podcast is established, and you want to make a bigger financial investment, think about renting some booth space. This assures that people who want to meet you will be able to find you easily. It also means that people who haven't heard of you will be more likely to come across you. The drawback is that this is a greater financial investment, and unless you bring a friend, you can end up stuck at that booth for the entire conference.

If you're in a big, crowded convention, not renting booth space, and want people to be able to connect your show with you personally from a distance, wear a t-shirt with your show art, or a pin. It's a good conversation starter.

Don't expect too much. Figure that you are helping people connect your face, your name, and your podcast. You'll also learn a lot about your show's topic, and get material for future episodes. If you have good manners and are pleasant to be around, it reflects well on your work. After you've swapped business cards or stickers, if you want to cross-market or cross-promote with them, send them an email after the convention.

Task List:

☐ Sign up for mailing lists of different conferences and conventions in your area.

☐ Choose a conference or two to attend.

☐ Plan your travel. You might want to concentrate on conferences which are easiest to attend.

☐ Design and purchase some business cards with a QR code on the back. Bring them with you.

☐ Pick out which workshops, lectures, or panel discussions are most important to you.

☐ Get there early so you don't miss anything.

☐ When you get home, make some notes of what you learned.

Related to: Merchandise, Online Communities,

Further Reading:

- How to Run Your Podcast Booth for Events

  > thepodcasthost.com/booth

- Podcast Events This Year

  > thepodcasthost.com/events

3. Partnering With an Event

Promoting your podcast at an event, convention, or conference is a great way to meet others with similar interests - from industry experts, to potential fans. You give some publicity to the conference itself, learn more about the topic, and invest in goodwill. Most importantly, an episode (or even part of one) recorded live at a conference is fun for your audience. If you can develop a good relationship with them, you could become the event's "official radio channel."

You may even meet conference guests who say they don't listen to podcasts, and convert them into your audience.

Additionally, there may be high-profile speakers you can interview for your podcast. Folks who would have been difficult to nail down as a guest if you were just reaching out to them online.

Type: Big Strategy

Time Required: One to three months, depending on the conference.

Podcast Level: At least 10 episodes

How to Do It

Research some conferences centered around your podcast topic. Find one or more which are simple to attend and high-profile. If one outweighs the other, decide which aspect is less of a risk. For example, if a conference is high-profile, though it requires expensive and time-consuming travel, it may be worth it for you to attend.

At least three months before the conference, email someone in the marketing department for the conference, and ask who's in charge of partnerships. They can tell you more about what's involved. Include your media kit, and mention the size of your audience. Effectively, you'd be promoting the conference, in exchange for admission and a place to set up your recording equipment. Let them know that you'll want to interview some of the conference speakers and guests.

Once you've got the green light, email the speakers you want to interview, and introduce yourself. Schedule some interviews. Let them know you're partnered with the conference, and you'll be promoting them.

Remember that conferences can be busy and hectic times for speakers. You will want to use a tool like Calendly, so they can select a time slot that fits with their schedule.

Your interview setup should be as simple as possible. Be aware of ambient noise. If you're recording from a promotional booth, you may want to have someone run your booth while you're recording, to answer any questions.

Record vox pops while you're there. Official speakers and guests at the conference aren't the only folks who have good info. Anyone who attends the conference could provide the next great insight for your podcast, or increase your audience. The concept is that you ask as many people at the conference the same short question. You can then hand out business cards with your show details on them, so they can be aware of the next episode.

Make sure your conference marketing team and interview guests know where they can hear the podcast, once it's published online.

Task List:

☐ Find some conferences related to your podcast topic.

☐ Decide which you can attend.

☐ Contact the marketing department, and ask about partnerships.

☐ Send your media kit (or a link to it) to the marketing department.

☐ Contact the speakers, and schedule interviews.

☐ Practice setting up your recording equipment for the conference.

☐ Get there early and interview your guests. Make sure you save a backup of your recordings, just in case.

☐ Take time to record vox pops.

☐ Thank the marketing team for the conference. Send an email to thank them, with links to your podcast, so they can download it at their convenience.

☐ Thank the individuals you interviewed. Send them an email to thank them, with a link to your podcast episode when it airs.

Related to: Helping Others To Help Yourself, Online Communities

Further Reading:

• How to Run Your Podcast Booth for Events

> thepodcasthost.com/booth

• Partnering with Conferences to Grow Your Interview Podcast

> thepodcasthost.com/partnerwithconferences

• How to Podcast from an Event: Live Broadcasting or Offline Recording

> thepodcasthost.com/podcastfromevent

4. Vox-Pops

Nope, it's not a new breakfast cereal. It's a journalism and/or marketing strategy. The name comes from vox populi, or voice of the people. It's a way of sketching out public opinion at a particular place and time. By asking a lot of different people the same question, you can get a lot of perspective on a bit of truth. This is also often used for comic effect by Jimmy Kimmel, and parodied by A Bit of Fry and Laurie. If you watch television, you have seen vox pops.

Type: Short Task

Time Required: A hour to record, an hour to edit

Podcast Level: 5-10 episodes, or when you're comfortable with your workflow.

How to Do It

Come up with a good episode topic, and one or maybe two related questions. Put together a remote recording rig which you can carry easily, such as a hand-held digital recorder and a pair of headphones. Go to a place with good foot traffic, but not so crowded that you'll have to shout to be heard. Think about places where your podcast topic would be relevant. If your podcast is about fly fishing, try the parking lot of a fishing spot, or partner with a bait and tackle shop. If your podcast is about quilting, check out a fabric shop.

Bring some of your podcast business cards with you so you can easily share details of where to find the show.

Participants do have to give you permission to record them. But you don't have to fill out a contract, just keep a recording of them saying "yes, you have my permission to record me."

If you see people who look like they might be interested, ask if they'd be up for participating in an interview for a podcast. Be aware that people might not be, and that has nothing to do with you: they might be on their way to work, headed home, or simply wanting privacy. Some people will want to participate. Keep it light, keep it quick, and give them a card so they can listen later.

Task List:

☐ Come up with a good episode topic, and one or maybe two related questions.

☐ Practice working with your remote recording rig, and saving the sound files.

☐ Get some business cards with your show information on them.

☐ Take your recording rig to a local spot with a reasonable amount of foot traffic. Bring a friend.

☐ Ask people if they'd be interested in participating in an interview for a podcast.

☐ Tell them about your podcast and offer them a card right away. That way, even if they say no, they've heard of your podcast.

☐ After you record them, thank them. Remind them that they'll be able to hear themselves on your podcast, and they should tell their friends.

Related to: Guerilla Marketing, Growth through Repurposing

Further Reading:

• The Best Podcast Digital Recorders on the Market

> thepodcasthost.com/digitalrecorders

• Why Record Your Podcast Outdoors?

> thepodcasthost.com/recordingoutdoors

5. Smaller Clubs and Societies

Where there's an interest, if you get two or more people who care about it together more than once, you have a club. If they add rules to the club, you can probably call it a society. You can almost guarantee that no matter how unusual your podcast's topic is, there is some kind of a club or society that gets together to talk about it, or some aspect of it. Those people are likely to be interested in your podcast.

For example, look at a podcast like *Organic Life*. You can certainly find clubs for people interested in farming, organic food, and gardening. A podcast like *Hostile Worlds* could be interesting to science and education groups.

Type: Short Task

Time Required: A hour or two

Podcast Level: 5 to 10 episodes

How to Do It

Your podcast isn't just about one thing. For example, a podcast about sewing has subtopics inside that topic, such as quilting, clothing design, fabrication, sewing gear, and so on. Make a list of topics that your show covers.

A quick search on Google will give you a sense of what's out there and where they meet (this brings us back to Meetup.com). For the aforementioned podcast, you might find sewing clubs, and you also might find costume design or quilting groups. You can visit a meeting and listen, and learn more about their goals and interests. Bring some cards with your podcast's info, in case someone asks about your show. You'll probably get a lot of food for thought for future episodes.

Caveat emptor: Walking in with the mindset of "I am here to promote my podcast" can alienate folks. Clubs and societies have their own agenda and history. You might accidentally walk in on the day they're voting for their board, or planning a fundraiser. Be respectful of that.

Task List:

☐ Get some business cards with your show's information.

☐ Make a list of topics and sub-topics related to your show.

☐ Search online for local clubs, societies or other groups interested in those topics.

☐ Contact the group and ask about attending a meeting (Where? When?)

☐ Go to the meeting and listen.

☐ When you're done, make some notes about what you learned.

Related to: Gaining New Visibility, Online Communities

Further Reading:

• Creating a 'Real Life' Podcast Community

> thepodcasthost.com/reallifecommunity

New Visibility

"We need old friends to help us grow old and new friends to help us stay young." - Letty Cottin Pogrebin

In podcasting, your primary concern should be to serve those who are already listening. But, once you've got that nailed down, how can you go about bringing some new ears into your audience? That's the purpose of this chapter. Here, you'll learn some tips and tactics that can help give those download numbers a nice boost!

1. **Being Interviewed on Other Shows**

2. **Using Traditional Media**

3. **Being Featured by Apple/iTunes**

4. **Awards & Competitions**

5. **Newsjacking**

6. **Promote a Milestone**

7. **Creating a Promo Trailer**

1. Being Interviewed on Other Shows

Other podcasts are an excellent place to promote your show, because 100% of the people you'll reach are already podcast listeners.

Doing an interview on another podcast in your niche lets you offer value, and win these listeners over to checking out your show. They get to hear your voice, your tone, and your delivery, before they've even heard your own podcast.

However, it isn't just as easy as emailing other podcasts and saying "Hey, interview me please!" So, let's look at how to actually make this strategy work.

Type: Big Strategy

Time Required: One week

Podcast Level: Unless you're well known for something outside of podcasting, the older your show is, the more chance of success you'll have here.

How to Do It

First up, have a think about the podcasts you'd like to be interviewed on. What great interview shows in your niche are out there, right now? Be sure to listen to a few episodes of any podcast you plan to reach out to.

When you decide on a specific podcast, reach out to them with a thorough proposal on what you can offer their listeners. What unique insights can you bring to the table? What value can you bring? Make this ALL about their audience!

Ultimately, what the podcast owner will want to hear, is;

- What you would like to chat about

- Why it would be useful and interesting to their audience

- Credibility - a little about you, and why you're well positioned to help

- The benefits their audience will get from it

- What keywords or search terms you are targeting, in relation to the episode title

- The ways you will share the episode to drive traffic to their show

Next up, instead of reaching out by email, create your proposal in audio, or - even better - video form. This personalised approach will be much more likely to resonate with the podcaster. It shows that you're not simply copying and pasting the same email to 100s of other shows. If you send someone a personalised video, the chances are, they'll watch it.

They'll also be able to hear your voice right away, and that you've got a good level of audio quality. This, combined with the value you promise to offer their audience, makes it difficult for them to ignore, and easy for them to say "yes".

There are alternative and more scalable options, though. Let's take a look at them.

Podcast Guest Services

You can put yourself out there as an available podcast interviewee on these useful platforms.

PodcastGuests.com

Podcast Guests links up those who want to find podcast interview guests with those who want to be podcast interview guests.

You can list yourself as an expert guest for $10 a month, on their basic package.

They also have a $29 a month premium package.

This allows you to

- Link to 3 websites instead of 1

- Be listed in 2 categories instead of 1

- Have your profile featured above "basic" members

- Be featured on social media on a rotating basis

- And have your profile featured in a rotating newsletter to over 20,000 subscribers

MatchMaker.fm

MatchMaker markets themselves as "like Tinder, but for podcasters".

You can use it either to find podcast guests, or to put yourself forward to be a guest on other shows.

It's totally free, and you can connect via your LinkedIn or Facebook accounts.

Podchaser Connect

Podchaser is often referred to as "the IMDb of podcasting". They have a range of excellent features for podcast listeners and podcasters alike.

The platform enables you to create your own profile, then link that profile to all the shows and episodes you've ever been involved in.

Their 'Podchaser Connect' feature at podchaser.com/connect - is marketed as "a new platform for strategically connecting experts and podcasts to create amazing content and grow audiences."

Alongside its custom profiles, you'll find data-driven matching between podcasters and potential guests, as well as detailed analytics and reporting.

Task List:

☐ Research and listen to podcasts relevant to your topic that you'd love to be interviewed on.

☐ Make sure they actually do interviews.

☐ Select 3 of them, and record short personalised videos to each presenter.

☐ Tell them what you like about their podcast.

☐ Tell them you'd love to be a guest on their show, and explain to them how you can serve their audience in this conversation.

Bonus Tasks:

• Sign up to PodcastGuests.com

• Sign up to Podchaser Connect

• Sign up to MatchMaker.fm

Further Reading:

• How to Be a Great Podcast Interviewee

> thepodcasthost.com/greatinterviewee

2. Using Traditional Media

Being mentioned in a newspaper or on the radio can give your podcast a nice boost in download numbers.

With traditional media such as these, audience numbers tend to be higher than podcasts, but audience engagement tends to be much lower.

With a compelling story, though, you can draw eyes or ears to the discussion around your podcast. Some of the folks reading or listening may be in your target audience, and those are the ones you're hoping will check out your show.

Type: Big Strategy

Time Required: One week

Podcast Level: At least 6 months old

How to Do It

Reaching out to traditional media outlets is generally done by creating a press release.

There actually needs to be a story that they'll be interested in, though. "Local woman has podcast" isn't really enough to capture even the most desperate journalist's attention.

Instead, you might want to take the approach of how you helped someone through your podcast. Your aim is to build a story that'll be of interest to a local paper or radio station.

This could involve a bit of listener involvement. For example, say someone does a podcast around marathon running for people with disabilities. Over time, they are going to collect some great case studies of how they've helped listeners to change their lives.

What Makes a Story?

Journalists tend to look for individual or "human" stories. Whilst "local podcaster helps people" might be more interesting than "local woman has podcast", it might still not be enough.

Imagine in our example, a story about 32 year old mum Jude, who lost her leg 5 years ago in a car accident, being inspired to start running by a podcast. Over time she continued to grow in confidence and strength, and recently ran the London Marathon.

It turns out that this podcast is run by someone in a journalists community, or within the geographical reach of their audience. Now they have a great story.

Of course, there's a few things to think about here before rushing off to write that press release. Firstly, a listener might've got in touch privately to update a podcaster on their life journey, but it would be wrong to contact the media without first discussing it with that person.

A conversation would be needed to explain what the podcaster would like to do, and to find out if the listener was okay with it. Were they also okay with being named, or would they prefer to remain anonymous? This is all just basic common sense to respect people's private lives, but it's worth mentioning.

Secondly, few of us can boast a listener story quite as noble as the one we've imagined up here, but it really doesn't need to be. Here are some examples.

- Podcaster helps listener launch own business after they were made redundant

- Podcaster helps listener in weight loss transformation

- Podcaster helps listener to learn Spanish and land dream tourism job

- Podcaster helps budding young author to win short story competition

Obviously, these are reliant on a few factors. Namely, that you've been running your show for half a year at the very least. You've had the time with your listeners to build such relationships, and have such an impact.

Your story doesn't need to be about a listener, though. It could be about you. Let's look at a few examples.

- Podcaster was a homeless alcoholic. Now he's helping others to stay sober

- Podcaster was given a month to live. Now she's helping others battle back from cancer

- Podcaster had a childhood speech impediment. Now they talk to hundreds

- Podcaster was rejected from art school. Now, podcast has helped them to sell first painting

Notice that these focus on a transformation. Journalists love that stuff, and it's the very basis of any story ever told.

So what's your story?

Writing a Press Release

To write a press release, you'd just write the story as if it were an article in a newspaper. Write in the third person, and use quotes - even if they are by yourself.

This makes a journalist's job super easy. They may choose to just use the entire press release as an article, verbatim. But it's more likely they'll rewrite sections and even contact you or anyone else mentioned for further questions and comments.

Task List:

☐ Think of a story you can build your press release around.

☐ Research the local radio stations and newspapers you plan to approach.

☐ Write your press release as if it were a published newspaper story.

☐ Find their "got a story?" contact on their website and send it over.

☐ Contact national radio stations and newspapers if you think they might be interested. They can only say No!

Further Reading:

• How to Write an Effective Press Release for Your Small Business

>thepodcasthost.com/pressrelease

3. Being Featured by Apple/iTunes

Despite the many hundreds of ways listeners can consume podcasts these days, Apple Podcasts/iTunes is still comfortably the biggest platform in the world. Over 60% of podcast listening happens there.

We know from our own data that when listeners want to find new content to listen to, around 40% of them take to searching their podcast listening app first.

Looking at those two stats, it isn't hard to conclude that if you were listed by Apple as a "featured" podcast, you'd likely pick up a few new listeners.

In fact, we know this ourselves first hand. In August 2017, one of our shows – Hostile Worlds – was featured on the front page of iTunes and Apple Podcasts. We'll link to the article where we break down our listening numbers from that period in the *Further Reading* section.

Type: Big task

Time Required: Months of planning - 10 minutes to submit your podcast

Podcast Level: 4 episodes or more

How to Do It

It's important to stress that there's no way to *guarantee* getting featured there. You need to show Apple you'll be publishing content that they reckon is feature-worthy. It's also important to stress that said episode **is not yet published**.

Apple will consider featuring a podcast on their front page if it's something topical or noteworthy. For example, if a show is going to have a famous guest on their show. This person must be widely famous – "someone your mum has heard of" – and not just "niche famous". This might be an author or musician with a new book or album. Apple sells these products, so they like to help market them.

A famous guest could also be a sports star ahead of a big final, or an actor around the time of a movie premier.

It doesn't need to be due to a guest though. It might be because your episode will focus on a major event or news story. That was the case with Hostile Worlds, and the Cassini Mission to Saturn.

Apple Submission Form

You'll find the Apple submission form at thepodcasthost.com/appleform

They're looking for at least 2 weeks lead time here, prior to the publishing of your noteworthy episode. They'd also like to know how you're going to promote and market this episode on their platform. This might include things like linking to your show in Apple on your episode post, and tagging them in social media posts around the episode.

Task List:

☐ Plan an episode that Apple may be interested in featuring.

☐ Fill out the submission form at least 2 weeks prior to the episode going live.

☐ Let Apple know how you'll be promoting and marketing the episode on their platform.

Further Reading:

• Apple Submission Form

> thepodcasthost.com/appleform Podcast Discovery Stats - thepodcasthost.com/discovery

• How Many Downloads Did We Get on the Front Page of iTunes/Apple Podcasts?

> thepodcasthost.com/itunesfrontpage

4. Awards & Competitions

"It's not the winning, it's the taking part" may be an old cliche, but there's some truth in it.

Awards and competitions aren't just a chance to win something. They're an opportunity for visibility too.

It can be useful to participate in a couple of awards or competitions each year. This can help you to spread the word about your show, expand your reach and network, and grow your audience.

Type: Big task

Time Required: 10 minutes each week to check for new opportunities. Half a day to prepare a submission.

Podcast Level: At least 6 months old

How to Do It

As with so many tips and tactics in this book, it'll depend a lot on your chosen niche or topic.

There are all kinds of awards, online and offline. The spectrum runs from podcast awards to regional business awards.

Some awards take the form of competitions too, where entrants will be asked to create something.

When you find an award or competition that looks interesting, have a look at the coverage around their previous years. What sort of places was it being shared, mentioned, or promoted? You might even choose to get in touch with some of the finalists (not just winners) to ask them about their thoughts and experiences.

You should check too, whether any award or competition you're considering charges a fee for taking part. Only you can decide if the money they are charging seems worth the visibility you're likely to gain from it.

Task List:

- ☐ Have a look for awards and competitions that fit the niche or topic of your podcast.

- ☐ Draw up a shortlist.

- ☐ Review content created around each one in previous years.

- ☐ Reach out to some of the previous year's finalists to find out their thoughts.

- ☐ Weight up time or cost commitments versus likely visibility from being involved.

- ☐ Set a short weekly task to check for new awards or competitions in your niche.

5. Newsjacking

Your podcast doesn't have to be tied to trending topics to be relevant. However, when current events relate to your podcast, it's worth pointing it out. This can net you some new audience and satisfy the current audience, encouraging them to share it.

Type: Regular Technique

Time Required: A few minutes a week, depending on the topic

Podcast Level: 5 episodes

How to Do It

Think of newsjacking as connecting with topics that are on many people's minds right now. You want to do this with some sensitivity. It's good to make the most of current events, but you don't want to exploit someone else's pain.

Start with something that is likely to be in the news for a while, so your episode is still relevant by the time you finish editing and release it into the world. For example, if you have a fly-fishing podcast, you could search online for news relevant to fly fishing enthusiasts, and do an episode about the remodelling and grand opening of the Catskill Fly Fishing Center and Museum.

Looking on Twitter and Google for trending topics is an excellent idea, though these tend to have a short shelf life in the cultural memory. Sometimes trending topics are a flash in the pan. By the time you get your episode edited, polished and uploaded, people may have forgotten about it.

Mention this on social media, and tag the news source, as well as whomever the news is about. In the aforementioned example, you might find the Catskill Fly Fishing Center recommending your podcast to their members.

What if your podcast is an audio drama? You can still benefit from sharing news and current events on social media, as long as they're relevant to your show.

Task List:

☐ Check news headlines for articles relevant to your show.

☐ Check Twitter and Google's trending topics.

☐ Find a few news items that are relevant. Research the news story on several different news sources, to make sure that it's real, and to get information from different perspectives.

☐ Plan an episode around at least one. Maybe you can get an interview with someone involved.

☐ Promote it on social media in conjunction with the news.

☐ Tag the news source.

Related to: Helping Others To Help Yourself, Contribute Constructively to Another Community.

6. Promote a Milestone

Setting goals for your podcast, meeting them, and celebrating them, is a great way to inject enthusiasm into a show that's been running for a while. The excitement generated can make new folks say, "what's this that I've been missing?"

Type: Big Strategy

Time Required: Depending on the milestone, about fifteen minutes to plan, fifteen minutes to execute, and fifteen to share.

Podcast Level: 10 episodes or more

How to Do It

Your fifth episode might not be a big deal, but ten is a nice round number. 4,628 downloads might not be something to celebrate, but surpassing 4,500 is a reasonable cause for a fancier social media post.

If you podcast in seasons, marking the end of one season, or the beginning of a new one is a memorable moment.

If you haven't achieved a satisfying milestone or goal yet, set one. What would be worth celebrating? Be realistic. This isn't the time for blue-sky thinking. If your podcast has 328 Twitter followers, what if you could get that number up to 500? Could you increase your number of downloads by 50%? Or, is there a nice round number ending in a couple of zeroes that's attainable?

You can make a montage episode to celebrate your milestone. You'll find a full guide on how to do that in the 'Helping Yourself by Helping Others' chapter.

Use a tool like Canva to make a special image to share on social media, celebrating your milestone. You can also use a tool like *Headliner* to make an audiogram to do the same thing.

When you set a podcast goal, meet it, and celebrate it, you renew your commitment. You can use this to invigorate and thank your audience. In turn, this can make people new to your podcast have a little FOMO and come over to press play.

Task List:

☐ Set a goal, like a number of downloads, or social media followers.

☐ Ask your audience to help you achieve this goal. For example, post on social media, asking them to recommend your podcast to friends. Include this goal in your call to action.

☐ Edit together a montage episode to celebrate your milestone. Pick out some of the best parts from previous episodes, and edit them together into a segment or episode.

☐ Ask your audience to contribute some recordings, answering a question related to your podcast. They can contribute recordings using a tool like Speakpipe, Dropbox or Google Drive.

☐ Put the audience recordings together into a montage episode.

☐ Use a tool like Canva to make a special image to share on social media, celebrating your milestone.

☐ Use a tool like *Headliner* to make an audiogram to celebrate your milestone.

Related to:. Helping Others To Help Yourself, Online Communities

Further Reading:

• Podcasting In Seasons

> thepodcasthost.com/seasons

• Celebrate Milestones & Grow Your Audience with a Montage Episode

> thepodcasthost.com/montage

- How to Make Great Podcast Cover Art

  > thepodcasthost.com/coverart

- A Beginner's Guide to Audiograms

  > thepodcasthost.com/audiograms

7. Creating a Promo Trailer

It's a good idea to create a short promo trailer for your podcast, for a couple of reasons.

Firstly, you can embed it on the front page of your website. That way, everyone who lands on your site can get an immediate taster of your content without the need to jump through any hoops.

Secondly, your trailer can easily be featured and played on other podcasts. This might be a show that invites promo trailer submissions. Or it might be a 'trailer swap' agreement between yourself and another podcast, to promote each other to your respective audiences.

Having your trailer easily accessible to all means that you might get promotion without even being aware of it too. If another podcaster likes your work, then can just download the audio and play it on their own show.

The only potential downside of having a promo trailer is if you have a bad one. The aim here is to help you make the most of the short amount of time you have to grab the attention of potential listeners.

Type: Short task

Time Required: A couple of hours to plan, record, produce, and publish

Podcast Level: From the beginning

How to Do It

Firstly, let's talk about length. I'd say that having two versions of your trailer, one at 30 seconds, and one at 60 seconds, will cover most bases. Some podcasts that request and play promo trailers will have length guidelines, and those tend to be about 30 seconds. If you want to create a 60 second version too though, you can use that one on your website homepage.

What Should Be in Your Promo Trailer?

You've always got creative license in podcasting, but there are a few bare essentials here. These may sound obvious, but you'd be surprised at how many trailers leave some of this stuff out.

The Name of Your Podcast

Yeah, you'll want to include that...

What's It About, & Who's It For?

Don't rely on the name of your show to tell people this valuable info. Tell them yourself. You can nail this down to a sentence or two.

A popular approach is to open with a question, like "are you a ___ who struggles with ___?, then join us on the ___ podcast where we help you ___."

Or "Have you ever wondered about ___?, or what about ___? Well these are just two of the topics you'll find us discussing each week on the ___ podcast."

Make sure your target audience knows this is the show for them, and that people who aren't your target audience know that it isn't for them.

Your Website

Like any good call to action, send them to one single easy to remember place. Preferably your own website. Don't say things like "look us up on Facebook" or "find us in Apple Podcasts" and run through a list of podcast directories. This is utterly redundant and a waste of valuable space.

It's good practice on your website to have a "Subscribe" page with links to everywhere you can be found.

You should make it easy for people to find, listen, and subscribe to your show, and the best way to do that is via your own website.

The Creative Bit: Tone & Personality

So, providing you've got the essential details in there, we don't want this to be a rigid formula that leaves every promo trailer sounding the same.

You want yours to sound unique, and that means getting creative. That's a challenge with such a short amount of time available, but you wouldn't be podcasting at all if you didn't have a creative streak in you. You'll manage!

Your promo trailer will be many listeners' first impressions of your show, so you want to set the mood right up front.

If you cover your topic in a lighthearted or comedic way, then you want to get that across to them.

Your audio quality (as well as any music or sound effects you use) will all filter into this just as much as what you actually say too.

If you run a highly-produced series, or pride yourself on your production values, then be sure to demonstrate that in your trailer.

Publishing

When uploading your promo trailer to your podcast feed, it's a good idea to backdate it to a date before the release of your first episode. That way, it'll keep your feed tidy, and can be easily found.

Once you've uploaded it, you can then embed it onto your website's homepage. You can also embed it anywhere else on the site that you think might be useful.

Anything to Avoid?

I've already mentioned the "find us in Apple Podcasts, Stitcher, Spotify, Soundcloud, Overcast..." thing as a no-no. So are there any other things you might want to leave out?

Explicit Language

Alright, I'm not saying don't have explicit language if it's integral to your mood or tone, but do consider that it might limit where your trailer will be played.

If you absolutely do need an explicit trailer, you might consider making an alternative clean version too.

Asking For Stuff

The only thing you want to ask people to do here is to listen to your podcast.

I've heard a couple of promo trailers over the years that managed to start asking for things like iTunes reviews and Patreon support. That's something you can talk to your *actual* listeners about, not your *potential* listeners.

Your trailer should be all about *them*, and what they'll get from listening.

Task List:

☐ Script yourself a 30 second trailer.

☐ Record, produce, and upload it.

☐ Publish it on your podcast feed.

☐ Backdate it to a date before your published your first episode.

☐ Embed it on your homepage and anywhere else on your website.

☐ Look for promo swap opportunities with other shows in your niche.

☐ You might consider making an extended 60 second version too.

Further Reading:

- Creating a Promo Trailer for Your Podcast

  > thepodcasthost.com/promotrailer

Organic Social Media

"Storytellers broaden our minds: engage, provoke, inspire, and ultimately, connect us." - Robert Redford

People have built relationships, influenced others and sold products long before there was Twitter and Instagram. Good manners, common sense, and meaningful conversation fueled Internet Relay Chat, Blogger and Live Journal, paving the way for influencer culture. By sharing content with some substance behind it, your podcast can attract attention like a pot on a stove: low heat, a long time, and a richer flavour.

1. Quote Images

2. Advanced Twitter Search

3. Live Video - Behind The Scenes

4. Tweet Your Reviews

5. Audiogram Highlights

6. Optimise Your Bio

7. Post Out Regular Questions

8. Use Tools to Make Regular Posting Easy

1. Quote Images

Images grab attention in social media posts, more so than text alone. If you combine an image with text (like a meme), you can use a quote from your show to hook potential listeners.

Type: Short Task

Time Required: Fifteen minutes to half an hour at most per image

Podcast Level: From the beginning

How to Do It

Any episode that you produce will have at least one great, short moment of dialogue. If you can use image editing software, you can add that line of text to a copy of your podcast logo, or an evocative image, and share it on social media. Include which episode it's from, and a link, and you can generate a bit of interest for your show. People who are new to your show will notice it more, and people who are already fans can share it easily, to motivate their friends to listen.

Listen to some of your favourite episodes from your podcast, and read over the transcripts. Find some pieces of dialogue from different episodes that feel like a good taste of your show.

Canva is a graphic design tool with a template specifically for making quote images. In their Social Media templates, they have dozens of Quote Image samples, where you can change the text, design elements, colours and so on. It's just like swapping out puzzle pieces. You can get started using Canva for free, but other graphic design tools are available.

If you keep the colour choices consistent with the colours in your podcast logo, this helps keep your branding consistent. It'll be easier for folks to associate the quote image with your podcast.

It's worth including a link to your "listen now" page, or to the episode page in your graphic. Try to make it as easy as possible for folks to become your new subscribers.

Task List:

☐ Pick out dialogue from different episodes to use.

☐ Make a quote image in Canva.

☐ Include a link to your "listen now" page, or to the episode page.

☐ Post it to your social media accounts.

☐ Encourage your followers to share the post.

Related to: Enabling Your Existing Audience, Online Communities

Further Reading:

• How To Use Creative Commons Images

> thepodcasthost.com/ccimages

• How To Make Great Podcast Cover Art

> thepodcasthost.com/coverart

2. Advanced Twitter Search

A lot of times, when people search for information online, they want answers based on personal experience (as opposed to advertising). Rather than searching on Google, they will type the question into a status update, and hope that one of their friends or followers will answer helpfully. In the case of Twitter, this can help you to know what kinds of questions people ask about your podcast's topic. Not only can you help people with answers, but hopefully they will be interested enough to try listening to your podcast.

Type: Short Task

Time Required: Fifteen minutes or less

Podcast Level: From the beginning

How to Do It

Twitter's advanced search function lets you customize your search to include certain words or phrases, exclude others, and select a language and/or date range. You can search not only for your podcast topic, but for phrases like, "does anyone know" or "can anyone recommend."

For example, if your podcast is about fly fishing, you can search for the term "fly fishing," and "does anyone know." The search results will show you tweets which include those phrases. Let's say you see a recent tweet that says, "Does anyone know of any good fly fishing spots in Montana?" you can try to answer their question helpfully.

Even if you have an entire episode devoted to the answer to their question, don't shove it on them. Just answer their question. If they respond positively, then you can offer a link to the podcast episode which could help.

More importantly, if you see the same question come up a lot, you know to devote more time and energy in your content planning to that topic.

Task List:

☐ Log into Twitter.

☐ Click on the search window. Search for your topic. A few results will come up, along with a link to "Advanced Search."

☐ Click on "Advanced Search."

☐ On the line for "all of these words," type in the topic you want to find questions about. Put it in quotes. For example, "fly fishing," as opposed to fly fishing.

☐ On the line for "this exact phrase," enter a question phrase, such as "does anyone know," or "can anyone recommend."

☐ Scroll to the bottom of the Advanced Search menu and select a date range. Keep your search results recent.

☐ Click Search.

☐ Read through the tweets, and see what's relevant. You might find people with similar interests to follow, or good insights you hadn't considered.

Related to: Helping Others To Help Yourself, Gaining New Visibility, Online Communities

Further Reading:

• Promote your Podcast with Twitter

> thepodcasthost.com/twitter

3. Live Video - Behind The Scenes

Let your audience see your process. Once you have your workflow settled, why not make a video to show your audience how you work?

Type: Short Task

Time Required: Fifteen minutes to an hour, once in a while

Podcast Level: From the beginning, or when you're comfortable with your workflow

How To Do It

You don't have to make a feature-length behind the scenes documentary. Put a camera on a tripod, or set it up securely, and make a video of your recording process. If you have your guest's permission, you can include them in the video. Most podcasters use behind the scenes content as a gift for backers in their monetization process. You can include it in your mailing list or social media posts if you like. Clean your recording area and make sure it looks nice. If you wrote any passwords on post-its and stuck them to your monitor, get them out of sight. Keep the video brief, informative, and fun. When you post the video to YouTube, you'll have the option to make the video unlisted. That means users can only see the video via a link that you control, not through YouTube's indexing.

Task List:

☐ While you're working, take a video of your process.

☐ Watch what you recorded and edit it.

☐ Post it to YouTube.

☐ Copy the link.

☐ Include the link in your behind the scenes content posts.

Related to: Growth Through Repurposing, Online Communities, Gaining New Visibility

Further Reading:

- YouTube Videos that Promote Your Content

  > thepodcasthost.com/youtubecta

- Content Stacking: Create Prolific Media & Fanatical Fans

  > thepodcasthost.com/contentstacking1

4. Tweet Your Reviews

Your reviews can help your podcast's status within the directory where the reviews are posted. Outside of that directory, they don't do much good, unless you show them off. Your reviews can convince new folks to listen. The way you post those new reviews rewards your current audience by making them feel part of your show.

Type: Short Task

Time Required: Five to fifteen minutes, once a month or week

Podcast Level: At any point in the process

How to Do It

Not all of your reviews will be positive, and not all of your positive reviews will necessarily be worth sharing. Some reviewers will click five stars and not type anything. Others will just write "great show," or something which is positive, but doesn't describe the podcast in any way. The reviews that are keepers are ones who mention something unique and memorable about your podcast. They might mention something the podcast did for them. These are PR gold, and do a lot of work for you.

To find your reviews more easily, you can also use a chart analytics service, such as Chartable, My Podcast Reviews, Podrover, or PodKite. These will show you reviews on the Apple Podcasts chart in other countries. Remember to check Podchaser, too.

Reviews are somewhat anonymous, especially on Apple Podcasts, because the reviewer's name comes up as a user handle. You might end up saying, "Thank you, @thx-11384lyf," and it seems odd, but they will know who they are. Whatever you do, express gratitude for the review.

Don't think of this as tooting your own horn or bragging. Think of it as a thank you note. By posting a screenshot, or the text of a review, you can thank the reviewer and other people who love your show. You also show independent reasons to listen, for people who are new to your podcast.

Task List:

- ☐ Check for reviews on Apple Podcasts and Podchaser.

- ☐ If you have a good, useful review, take a screenshot.

- ☐ Edit it so it looks nice.

- ☐ Post the screenshot on social media.

Related to: Enabling Your Existing Audience, Directories

Further Reading:

- How to Keep Track of Your Podcast Reviews

  > thepodcasthost.com/trackyourreviews

- How Do I Get More iTunes Reviews?

  > thepodcasthost.com/getmorereviews

5. Audiogram Highlights

Audiograms combine images, text, and audio to create a social media post. they are as memorable and attention-grabbing as video, without being as time-consuming or data-heavy. WNYC created an open-source code to accomplish this means of podcast promotion, and there are other options available to you now, too.

Type: Short Task

Time Required: One hour

Podcast Level: From the beginning

How to Do It

The open-source code that WNYC created was intended to be a free resource for podcasters to use to promote their work. It's great, but it can be confusing for people who don't know how to code. Fortunately, *Headliner* has created an app which guides you through the process. The free version lets you make a certain number of audiograms per month. Depending on the social media platform for which you intend to make your audiogram, the size constraints vary. However, you can use the same content with different aspect ratios or time limits for different platforms.

Figure out what section of your podcast you want to highlight. Much like quote images, an audiogram is a sample of a moment from your podcast. In this case, instead of a line or two of text, you're using a few seconds to a few minutes of audio.

Decide on the art you want to use. For consistency, you probably want to use your podcast logo. However, you can certainly use whatever art you want, as long as it fits with *Headliner*'s size requirements.

Including closed-captioning is a wise choice. Many people browse social media with the sound turned off, and don't turn the sound on unless they're curious about a particular post. If you include closed-captioning (well done: you make your post more accessible), go through and edit it for accuracy.

Headliner's mobile app honestly makes it easy for you to promote your show from your phone. You could do this while you're waiting for a coffee order or sitting in a park.

Task List:

- ☐ Go to *Headliner*'s website and sign up for a free account.

- ☐ Use the Audiogram Wizard and type in your podcast's name or RSS feed.

- ☐ Select the portion of your podcast episode that you want to share.

- ☐ Follow the Audiogram Wizard instructions to create your audiogram.

- ☐ If you use closed-captions, proofread and edit them for accuracy.

- ☐ Check the audiogram to make sure it's just right.

- ☐ Download a copy for your archives.

- ☐ Post the audiogram to social media.

- ☐ Make sure that the post includes a link to your podcast website.

- ☐ Encourage your followers to share the post.

Related to: Enabling Your Existing Audience, Advertising Your Podcast, Online Communities, Growth Through Repurposing

Further Reading:

- How to Make and Use Audiograms

    > thepodcasthost.com/audiograms

- Publishing Your Podcast on YouTube

  > thepodcasthost.com/publishtoyoutube

6. Optimise Your Bio

Whether you're on Twitter, Instagram, or any other social media platform, you should spend a bit of time optimising your account's bio section.

We know for a fact (according to our 2020 podcast discovery survey - find it at ThePodcastHost.com/Discovery) that your podcast's description is THE most important thing potential new listeners look at when weighing up whether or not to hit play. It makes sense then, that your bio on social media shouldn't simply be written as an afterthought.

Of course, social media follower counts and engagement don't automatically translate to podcast listeners. But, with a bit of thought put into your bio on social, you should be able to pique the interest of folks who fall into your target audience category.

Type: Short Task

Time Required: 30 minutes

Podcast Level: From the beginning

How to Do It

Some people love social media, and will create an account for themselves, an account for their podcast, and, probably, an account for their cat whilst they're at it.

Others prefer to take a minimalist approach and will only use their personal account. However, depending on your life or work outside of podcasting, you might have no space to even mention your show in your existing social bios.

So firstly, consider creating a dedicated podcast account on the social media platform you use and like the most. In the *Use Tools to Make Regular Posting Easy* task (this chapter), you'll find various options to make managing multiple social accounts easy.

A dedicated podcast account is much more obvious to those who see it. And that's before they've even read your bio.

If the name of your show tempts your target audience to click on your account, then your bio can do its job to convert them into a fully-fledged podcast subscriber.

You should approach this in the same way you approach all of your content creation - you make it all about *them*. You make it very clear that this is a podcast for ____, about ____, and you're going to help them to ____.

You should only add in one link, and you do that in the dedicated 'Link' or 'Website' section, not your bio. Your bio is precious space to convince potential listeners to actually click that link.

Send them to your website (if you have one), or at least, a dedicated page where they can find subscribe links on all the major directories. Don't put your Apple Podcasts link in here, unless you want to alienate the entire half of the world who use Android devices.

Also, avoid linking to Patreon, or any other "support us" platform. The job here is to win over new listeners, first and foremost. Once they've actually hit play, they'll hear all about your support avenues in the episodes themselves.

If you podcast in a traditionally "non-techy" niche, you might mention in your bio that you can "listen and subscribe for free". Many non-podcast listeners will have no idea that they won't have to pay for it, so make that clear.

An alternative selling point is to say something like, "available everywhere podcasts are found". This assures potential listeners that they can hit play on the apps they already use and love. It says to them "we've made this easy for you", and they'll subconsciously appreciate that.

Task List:

- ☐ Consider creating a dedicated account for your podcast on your favourite social platform.

- ☐ Make your bio all about your listener. What's the show about? Who's it for? What will they get from listening?

- ☐ Add in one link only. Send them to a dedicated 'subscribe' page with links to the top directories.

- ☐ Consider adding the selling points "listen and subscribe for free", or "available everywhere podcasts are found".

Related to: Growth Through Repurposing, Gaining New Visibility, Use Tools to Make Regular Posting Easy

7. Post Out Regular Questions

Asking questions of your audience can inspire feedback and participation. If you do it on a consistent basis, it makes your audience think of you as a source of inspiration. It feels good to answer a question, even if there is no particular correct answer, and feel that one's contribution is valuable.

Type: Regular Technique

Time Required: Maybe fifteen minutes, once a week or so

Podcast Level: From the beginning

How to Do It

Ask your audience a question related to each podcast episode. You can do this in your call to action, in your social media posts, show notes, or all of the above. Specificity teases a bit of the episode content. Some podcasters put simple opinion polls on their Twitter posts. Discussing the answers you receive in future episodes injects some energy into your podcast content.

Task List:

☐ For each episode topic, think of a question for your audience.

☐ Post the question on a consistent basis (one per episode) on your social media, show notes, and website.

☐ Mention each question in your call to action.

☐ Make sure that folks can answer your question. Responding on Twitter is as easy as replying, but in your CTA or show notes, you'll want to include your contact link.

☐ When you get answers, compile them into one note.

☐ Discuss the answers on your next episode, and thank people who responded.

☐ Think about how the answers can help you plan future episodes.

Related to: Enabling Your Existing Audience, Being Found Easily, Online Communities, Growing your Audience by Knowing your Audience, Growth through Repurposing

8. Use Tools to Make Regular Posting Easy

You might feel that you don't have time for social media, but that doesn't mean you need to miss out on its potential benefits. Social media automation tools can make sure your content shows up, while keeping you safe from distraction, and on schedule. These tools can even tell you how much of an impact your social media posts are having. Another benefit is that, if you run more than one social media account (say, one for your podcast, one for your personal life and one for your professional life), these kinds of tools can keep those from getting mixed up.

Type: Regular technique

Time Required: An hour to pick out and set up, then a few minutes a week

Podcast Level: From the beginning

How to Do It

A social media automation tool is software which posts on Twitter, Facebook, and similar sites for you, requiring little to no human interaction. They have analytics to show you how many views and clicks each post gets.

Here are a few of the best.

Hootsuite and Buffer are a couple of tools which let you plan your social media posts in advance, and schedule when you want them to appear.

Later is a tool specifically for Instagram, which also allows you to manage comments on your posts.

An interesting social media automation tool is MeetEdgar. Not only will it post on the schedule you choose, but also it will find relevant content for you to post. Need a current event or a 'this day in history?' Edgar can find it for you. It also has a workaround for

Twitter's rules about variations in post content, to make sure your posts stay fresh.

BuzzSumo is very popular because it checks for trending topics, and can help you build relationships with other influencers.

Whatever tool you choose, take the time to test-drive it and kick the tires. Sign up for the free trial, then set a reminder in your phone to decide whether or not to keep the tool, about a day or two before the trial ends. You don't want to discover that your #WednesdayWilderness posts are coming out on Friday, or the inside joke you wanted to share with your college friends is visible to the entire world.

Task List:

☐ Try out BuzzSumo (7-day free trial) , Meet Edgar (1-month free trial), Hootsuite (30-day free trial) and/or Buffer (14-day free trial).

☐ Schedule at least one social media post per day for 3-5 days, but no more than three.

☐ See what your engagement looks like, how many views and clicks your posts get.

☐ If the tool will suggest content for you to post, try it. See what the post engagement is like.

☐ Before the free trial is over, weigh the cost of the tool against the amount of time you've saved, and how much your posts engage people. If you have new subscribers, great!

Related To: Growth Through Repurposing, Being Found Easily

Guerrilla Marketing and Merchandise

"The brain uses images to help the conscious mind understand." -
Jay Conrad Levinson

Guerrilla Marketing is a fantastic and fun way to market your podcast. This low or no-cost unconventional advertising strategy allows you to engage with the public on a more personal and memorable level. In this chapter, we'll cover a few Guerrilla Marketing options that might work well for you, and your podcast.

1. **Leave a Business Card in a Book**

2. **Stickers or Magnets**

3. **Coasters/Beer Mats**

4. **QR Codes**

5. **Sell T-shirts and Other Merchandise**

1. Leave a Business Card in a Book

Books may be very old, and podcasts very new, but both have a lot in common. They're created with a target audience in mind. This book has a target audience. Your podcast also has a target audience. So why not promote your podcast in books that share your overarching theme or topic?

Type: Short Task

Time Required: One day, or ongoing strategy

Podcast Level: At any time

How to Do It

Okay, so this was much more straightforward back in the days when most readers used libraries. If you still have an active library local to you, and it's something you think folks in your target audience are using, then this is a good place to start.

But, what about the business cards themselves? This is a whole topic of its own. And to be honest "business card" is a pretty stuffy and boring term, isn't it? They're really just small flyers, in this instance.

If you don't already have cards for your podcast, then they should be approached in the same way as any advert for your show. The 'hook' is key, here. If someone opens a book on money saving, and a card drops out that just says "Listen to Jim's Podcast!", they're going to ignore it.

But if a card drops out that says "Learn how to save $400 a year on your food shopping, free, on Jim's Podcast" then that might just capture their attention.

We look at this in more detail in the "Flyers" section of the Advertising chapter, so won't repeat it all here. The bottom line is, the success of this technique will largely depend on the content and design of your card.

Another factor is, obviously, the topics of the books you're sticking cards in. A podcast on skateboarding will be unlikely to pick up any new listeners by having a lot of cards stuck into books on diet and nutrition, for example.

It's totally topic dependent, but self-help books will work well for many podcasters. As will biographies and autobiographies.

If you don't think the library approach will work, you might consider a local bookstore. Such a strategy is, of course, entirely at your own risk. The owner or staff might not take too kindly to you doing this, if they were to catch you. (Pro tip: you might plead the classic, "it's just a free bookmark!" defence).

A much smaller-scale way of doing this, is to sell any books you own on Amazon or Ebay, and pop a card into those before you post them out to their new owners.

Task List:

☐ Refer to the "Flyers" chapter of the Advertising chapter for guidance on your card design. The key here is the 'hook' that makes folks want to find out more.

☐ The books you use should be relevant to your podcast's niche or topic.

☐ Decide where you'll find books in your topic - a library? A bookstore?

☐ Stick cards into books you don't own at your own discretion. The book's owner may not take kindly to it, if they catch you.

☐ Consider selling books you own on Amazon and Ebay. Stick a card in these before posting them out.

Related to: Flyers (Advertising Your Podcast)

2. Stickers or Magnets

Stickers are the ultimate guerrilla marketing tool. They're like little ads for your podcast that can pop up anywhere, and they can last for a long time. Magnets can be used in similar ways, and can help keep you on the right side of the law, too.

Type: Ongoing task

Time Required: One month from design through to creation and delivery. Ongoing strategy to distribute.

Podcast Level: At any time

How to Do It

Stickers and magnets are a little different from flyers and cards. They're often more about the visual design, rather than the info. It's popular for podcasters to simply use their cover art as their sticker design. You could squeeze a domain onto there, but adding in any more text could be overkill. TeePublic.com is a great place to buy stickers and magnets.

We have an affiliate link for TeePublic which you are more than welcome to use (or not!) - and that's at thepodcasthost.com/teepublic

There are two approaches to marketing your podcast with stickers and magnets. The first, is to simply give them away to people. You might do this at a conference or event in your niche. You can even use the business card strategy and leave them in books (don't stick anything to the book, obviously!).

The point is, most people like stickers - even if they've never heard of the brand behind it. Give someone a sticker, and they're unlikely to chuck it away. They're also quite likely to stick it somewhere. This could be anything from the back of a laptop, to a dedicated "sticker wall" in their house or office.

Another popular place to see stickers is someone's fridge. That's why magnets can be equally useful - you're subconsciously telling them where to put it.

Don't underestimate the power of getting your logo onto someone's fridge. They'll see it every single day for years. Your podcast artwork will be burned into their brain - figuratively speaking, of course :-)

The second approach to using stickers and magnets is the DIY approach. Remember, it's your own responsibility to stay on the right side of the law here. Magnets may be tolerated more than stickers, because they're easily removed. Someone might even take it home with them.

If you do find a place with stickers plastered everywhere, then adding one to the mix is likely going to be okay. Pubs and bars that act as music venues are usually plastered in stickers. Of course, whether or not this is worthwhile totally depends on your show topic. The "I Really Hate Beer and Live Music" podcast might not find so many listeners using this technique.

Putting up stickers and magnets in various places is a "scattergun" approach where most people who'll see them aren't your target audience. Depending on your topic too, you might see it as unprofessional or even damaging. If that's the case, you should still consider giving them away to let listeners make their own minds up. If you make it onto someone's fridge, you've found a listener for life!

Task List:

☐ Decide on the design for your sticker or magnet. Most people opt for their podcast cover art.

☐ Use TeePublic.com to create them. If you want to sign up via our affiliate link it's thepodcasthost.com/teepublic.

☐ Plan to attend some events and conferences where you can give them away for free.

☐ Consider putting some stickers and magnets in public places at your own discretion.

Further Reading:

- Guerrilla Marketing for Podcasters

  > thepodcasthost.com/guerrilla

3. Coasters/Beer Mats

This is a "helpful" way of distributing your podcast logo or branding around pubs and bars in your area. A little cardboard coaster is a useful thing in these places. They help keep the table dry, and some folks even collect them. If your design is intriguing enough, a person resting their glass on one may pull out their phone and subscribe to your podcast there and then.

Type: Ongoing task

Time Required: One month from design through to creation and delivery. Ongoing strategy to distribute.

Podcast Level: At any time

How to Do It

The starting point is your coaster design. What are you going to put on there to catch people's eye?

Your podcast logo can be a good choice here, just like with stickers or magnets. But, unlike those, you have a bit more time with the person looking at your coaster. They're also up close to it, so it doesn't need to work in an at-a-glance sort of way.

I actually recommend getting yourself 2-4 different designs. A typical bar or pub table sits 4 people, so you can leave 4 different coasters which could even spark some discussion amongst the folks who sit there next.

Could you create one using a quote from a podcast review? Or, from yourself or an interview guest on the show? You can use humour or intrigue to make the person looking at it want to find out more. As always, it comes down to your own brand and tone, as well as your target audience.

You should always have your podcast's name on each coaster. Get your URL on there too. Make sure the people who want to find out more, actually can.

Cardboard coasters are relatively cheap to have made. Many online printing services offer this service, and you'll generally pick up bundles of 100 to 250 with each design.

Next comes the distribution. I use this guerrilla marketing tactic myself; I'll shove a stack of them in my jacket pocket if I'm heading on a day out somewhere. Each time I'm in a pub, I'll stick coasters under all of our glasses at the table. When we leave, other folks will sit there, and who knows? One might even go on to become the show's biggest fan.

You can also harness the power of your listeners by running a competition. Ask them to take a picture of their drinks proudly sitting on your coasters when they're out somewhere. You can run a hashtag for this so everyone can see each other's pictures, too.

This is a fun way to market your podcast, because you never know who's going to sit down and start studying your "ad" next. Also, it's a great excuse to get some friends together and go for a drink one weekend!

Task List:

☐   Have 2-4 different types of coaster design made.

☐   Use your logo, but also consider things like quotes from reviews or from the show itself.

☐   Remember to have the podcast name, or even a URL on them.

☐   Each time you're going to be in a cafe, pub, or bar, take some with you.

☐   Put them under the glasses or cups on your table as you drink.

☐   When you leave, leave them for the next people who'll sit there.

☐ Consider running listener competitions to see how many bars around the world you can get photos of your coasters "in action".

Related to: Stickers & Magnets, Leave a Business Card in a Book

Further Reading:

• Guerrilla Marketing for Podcasters

> thepodcasthost.com/guerrilla

4. QR Codes

You may have seen QR (quick response) codes before. Marketers use them on food labels, signs, and business cards. They look like little black and white checkerboards, gone awry. It's a unique symbol that your smartphone's camera can read and translate into a web address. Most smartphones' operating systems have this function in their camera's software now. However, QR code reader apps are often free.

Type: Short task

Time Required: One hour

Podcast Level: From Episode 1

How to Do It

When you make promotional materials, such as stickers or business cards, you can include a QR code in your image or text. This way, not only do people have a tangible result of a conversation with you (the card or sticker), they can act on it easily. All they have to do is scan the QR code with their smartphone's camera. A notification will pop up, saying, "this links to (your podcast website)."

You should have one page on your web site that briefly describes your podcast, and how to listen, in a nutshell. It should have the simplest possible summary, and links to it in different directories. You want to make sure that the user can sample your podcast in the fewest possible number of clicks. If you use embedded players, you can embed a trailer on that page as well. Let's say the URL for that page is your podcast.com/listen-now.

Many business card and sticker designers include QR codes as an option in the design process. Take <u>Moo.com</u>, for example. Their website walks you through the process of designing the business cards, and generating the QR code. You enter your podcast.com/listen-now. When the website generates the QR code, you just add it to the overall design, like an image.

Task List:

☐ Set up or optimize your website's "Listen Now" page.

☐ Include QR code in design when having business cards, stickers, or flyers made.

Related to: Stickers & Magnets, Leave a Business Card in a Book, Flyers (Advertising)

Further Reading:

• QR Codes: A Great Way to Promote & Share Your Podcast

> thepodcasthost.com/qrcodes

5. Sell T-shirts and Other Merchandise

Selling t-shirts or other merchandise is a little bit tougher, because, obviously, you have to sell it. The payoff is that not only can you recoup the money you put into the merch by selling it, but, again, your buyer becomes a mobile billboard for your podcast. If you do this right, you can add value to your listeners' experience with good merch, delivered properly. If you don't, you could end up with a closet full of boxes of stuff nobody wanted to buy.

Type: Big Strategy

Time Required: An hour to create, the turnaround time of the supplier, and then a few minutes to sell

Podcast Level: 10 episodes

How to Do It

Print on-demand merchandise is the saving roll of the independent artist. Rather than having to print up batches of shirts, water bottles or whatever, store them, display them and try to sell them, your audience can pick out a design and item that they want, in the size and colour they need. You can promote the shop in your call to action, website, and social media.

Since this is much simpler than the traditional print/store/display/sell chain, you can afford to have unusual or niche designs. You don't have to have merch which only has your podcast logo. If your podcast has an episode with some particularly brilliant, trenchant or exciting content, build a design around it.

Some considerations: you should check through the policies of different print on demand companies, and decide which is right for you. Read through their design specifications. What size and dpi does your image have to be? Is the process easy for you? Is the time you put in worth it to you? Do they have customizable storefronts? Can you have sales or discounts for your audience? Make sure this doesn't take up too much of your time, and that it's easy to use.

Right now, enamel pins are de rigueur. They're relatively inexpensive to have made, look good, and people like to collect them. More importantly, one size fits all.

Task List:

☐ Check out several print on demand companies, such as Teepublic, Redbubble, and Teespring.

☐ Read through their design specifications.

☐ Make a version of your podcast logo that conforms to those specifications.

☐ Upload it and design a product.

☐ When you have merchandise ready to sell, promote this on your social media, website, and in your call to action.

Related to: Live Events, Enabling Your Existing Audience

Further Reading:

• Guerrilla Marketing for Podcasters

> thepodcasthost.com/guerrilla

• How To Make Great Podcast Cover Art

> thepodcasthost.com/coverart

Growth Through Repurposing

"Often when you think you're at the end of something, you're at the beginning of something else."

– Fred Rogers

Tapas once was meant as samples of an inn's full menu. Spanish innkeepers would offer samples of ham or other cured meats, as a "tapa" or lid across the guest's glass, to protect their drink from flies and dust. Since the meat was salty, it would tempt the traveller to order more to consume. If you think about your podcast content like a full meal, there are ways to repurpose it, like tapas. Here, potential listeners can get tastes of your work to decide if your show is right for them. In this section, we'll look at different ways of packaging material from your podcast, so that people who aren't already committed can try it out.

1. **Live Broadcasting**

2. **Blogging Your Episodes**

3. **Milestone Episodes**

4. **Posting Video Versions of Episodes**

5. **Social Media Stories**

6. **Compile and Share an Ebook**

1. Live Broadcasting

A live episode of your podcast will always seem more exciting, because of the audience reactions and involvement. You can do this by recording your podcast live in front of an audience, or you can do it online, with software You can allow the audience to ask questions, or just let them engage with each other in the chatroom.

Type: Regular Technique

Time Required: About the same amount as it takes for you to record, edit and upload an episode

Podcast Level: 20 or more episodes

How to Do It

There are a few ways to do this. The most labour-intensive, obviously, is the method that we discussed in the *Running Live Events* chapter. What's great about this is that if your mic picks up positive reactions from the audience (i.e., applause, laughter), it makes your episode feel more alive and urgent. However, there are more variables in play, and this might not be your cup of tea.

Another way to present in front of your listeners is to use conferencing software, such as ECamm, Google Meet, or Zoom. This makes you more human to your audience, and can increase their emotional investment in your show.

Many podcasters joke about having "a face for radio" and say that they went into podcasting so that they didn't have to worry about what they look like. The truth is, the more positive experiences your audience has where they can see your face, the more they associate your face with feeling positive, and it makes you seem more good-looking to them.

If you enjoy using a chat-based communication tool, like Slack or Discord, you can invite your audience to join you on a Slack or Discord channel, while you record.

You can allow your audience to chat with you and ask questions. You can also just let them have a running commentary. Sometimes people who are all fans of the same thing like to chat with each other while the recording is taking place.

You'll need to mention the live episode and the opportunity to chat at least three times for audiences to have it stick in their minds. Make sure that you plan the live episode with enough time to mention it in your episode Call to Action at least three times, and on social media at least three times.

In a post on your website, include the information about how people can participate in the chat. If you're using Discord, Slack, Zoom or Google Meet, have them send an email (or include a mail link) to get on a list for the login link and password. This way, you have a mailing list, and you know that the participants are invested enough in your podcast to send you an email. Then, a few days before, send out an email with the link to your audience.

Schedule the recording for a time that's best for you, but be conscious of time zones. If most of your listeners are in a time zone five hours ahead of you, starting your recording at 9pm probably won't get much participation.

Be aware that sometimes internet trolls sign up for and log into live events with a live chat so they can post rude statements that have nothing to do with anything (the practice is sometimes called "zoom bombing"). While it's unlikely that this will happen, know how to momentarily pause the chat function and block a participant. You can always edit this part out before you upload the recording as a podcast episode.

When you record, be aware of your audience participating, but don't let them drive the discussion (unless, of course, that's your plan!)

Your audience will, more than likely, ask questions about your podcast's topic that you hadn't considered, and spark ideas for future episodes. Plus, you'll have an episode invigorated by audience participation.

Task List:

☐ Take a look at Ecamm, Zoom, and Google Meet. Decide which one is best for you.

☐ Practice using it with a few friends.

☐ Decide what episode topic(s) you'd like to record live.

☐ Check the geographical data of your downloads, to figure out what time zone the majority of your listeners live in.

☐ Plan a date and time to record live. Give yourself enough time that you will be able to mention it in at least three episodes.

☐ Post the information about the live recording, and how to join, on your podcast website.

☐ Promote the live recording on your podcast's social media, and in the Call to Action of at least three episodes.

☐ A day or two before, compile the list of people who asked to join the live recording. Send them the official invitation, with the login information.

☐ Set up your conferencing software, and record your episode.

☐ Before you finish recording and wrap up, thank them for participating.

Related to: Attending Live Events, Live Recording

Further Reading:

• Live Broadcasting for Podcasts

> thepodcasthost.com/livepod

2. Blogging Your Episodes

Comprehensive blog posts of your episodes may seem like overkill. However, not everyone processes information the same way. Some folks may need a text or visual element to help them understand and act on your content. With good show notes, transcripts, and text that complements rather than replaces your podcast, you can make your podcast easier for your audience to digest and share.

Type: Regular Technique

Time Required: 15-30 minutes per episode

Podcast Level: From the beginning.

How to Do It

Your audience isn't only made up of people who listen. There are people interested in your podcast's topic who are hearing impaired, or have auditory processing problems. Maybe they simply don't enjoy listening to things, but would still enjoy your topic and ideas.

Along with your blog posts, transcripts help people who can't listen to your show to enjoy and share it. They also help listeners to better understand your show, and reviewers to write about it. There are different ways to get your episodes transcribed. You can do it yourself, with some simple tools. You can hire a freelancer. You can try a service; there are many right now, and costs vary. Choosing the best way to transcribe your podcast has a lot of variables: time, effort, cost, and the kind of business you want to support.

No matter what, a lack of episode transcripts prevents a lot of people from engaging with your content at all.

You don't have to include the whole transcript in each episode's blog post. You can have it on a separate page, or in a Google Drive folder, linked from the relevant blog post.

Blog posts provide a way for your podcast to be found more easily via SEO. Think of each episode's blog post as a visual companion to your audio content. It's another way for your audience to enjoy it and share it with others.

Task List:

☐ Create a blog post for each episode.

☐ Use whatever visual resources (photos, graphs, illustrations, etc.) enhance your podcast episode for each blog post.

☐ Take a look at some transcription services to see which one meets your needs.

☐ When considering a transcription service or freelancer, consider turnaround time, cost, and accuracy.

☐ When you have transcripts for each episode, link to them on the relevant blog post.

☐ Include social sharing links on each blog post, and that episode's call to action.

Related to: Enabling Your Existing Audience, Share Buttons

Further Reading:

• How To Get Your Show Transcribed

> thepodcasthost.com/transcription

• Blogging vs Podcasting: Which Content Method?

> thepodcasthost.com/blogvspod

• How to Link to and Share a Podcast

> thepodcasthost.com/linktopodcast

3. Milestone Episodes

When you have good clips from previous episodes, you can create a special montage episode. This celebrates what you've achieved so far. It evokes nostalgia in your established listeners, and shows how far you've come. It can also give new folks a point of entry to your podcast as a whole.

Type: Big Strategy

Time Required: Half a day to plan, script, and edit

Podcast Level: After a solid round number of episodes, say 50 or 100

How to Do It

Your montage episode will be as unique as your show's intention. One way is to recap the highlights of your podcast so far, using the "best" clips from different episodes. You can also select clips based around a theme.

Edit this into one continuous episode, with your usual intro, outro, and call to action.

Task List:

☐ Choose which type of montage episode you want to make.

☐ Pick out clips from your previous recordings which best suit that kind of montage.

☐ Edit together as a single episode, with your usual intro, CTA and outro.

☐ Publish.

Related to:

Montage Episodes (Helping Yourself By Helping Others)

Further Reading:

- How to Make A Montage Episode

  > thepodcasthost.com/montage

4. Posting Video Versions of Episodes

Your podcast recordings can be easily repurposed into short video clips. This is a great way to make use of your podcast trailer, or any moment that stands on its own as a good example of your podcast. Video clips can be shared on social media, particularly well on services such as Instagram. These visual clips can be used to convert the people who "never listen to podcasts" (but can be easily distracted by YouTube) into your audience.

Type: Regular Technique

Time Required: About the same amount of time as you spend on each episode.

Podcast level: From the beginning

How to Do It

If you film every podcast recording, you can easily repurpose your content into a video clip. 30 seconds or 60 seconds is enough. You'll end up with a lot of video footage, which you may want to repurpose into a montage trailer to celebrate a milestone, or to revisit to celebrate an anniversary and see how far you've come.

You don't have to record video of every podcast recording, though. If you wait until you have several episodes recorded and published, and feel confident, then try it. You don't necessarily have to play to the camera. Don't be distracted. Just concentrate on making great content. Many people use visual art, combined with their audio, instead of a video of themselves recording.

If you and your co-host and/or interview guest record remotely, it can be even easier to make video of your recording process. ECamm Call Recorder and TalkHelper for Skype, and Zoom all record video. You can easily repurpose this into some great guest answer montage episode.

Another way to share video of episode highlights is to make an audiogram. You can combine a clip of your video with visual art, a waveform, and closed-captioning, to make a short visual nugget of your show. These tend to be really sticky, as Malcom Gladwell would say: they catch people's attention, they're memorable, and they attract clicks. *Headliner* is a free app which can walk you through the process of making audiograms.

Making a video of your trailer and posting it to YouTube is a good way to share it outside of the usual audio channels.

You can embed video or audiograms into social media posts, blog posts, and Facebook ads.

Don't forget that advertising can be targeted, so your video can end up doing a lot of work for you over time.

Task List:

☐ Figure out how you can fit a video camera (whether on your phone, in your desktop, or on a tripod) into your recording setup, unobtrusively.

☐ Alternatively, use call recording software that also records video.

☐ Practice video recording yourself while recording your podcast.

☐ Check out *Headliner* and try their Audiogram Wizard.

☐ Find the best clips of your podcast, and use them to make an audiogram or video clip.

☐ Embed the resulting videos into social media posts, and share them to promote your podcast.

Related to: Advertising Your Content, Organic Social Media

Further Reading:

• Best Call Recording Apps for Online Call and Remote Recording

> thepodcasthost.com/callrecordingapps

- How To Make and Share Audiograms

  > thepodcasthost.com/audiograms

- How To Grow Your Podcast With Facebook Ads

  > thepodcasthost.com/facebookads

5. Social Media Stories

What if you could post an image or short video promoting your podcast, pinned to the top of your followers' social media feed? If you've used Instagram or Facebook, you've probably seen social media 'stories.' These are images people share that disappear after 24 hours, but can be saved into a slideshow by the user.

Social media stories can combine images, text, video and audio to share a moment of your life. A particularly interesting example of this is the Instagram account, @Eva.Stories. Each part is a moment in the life of a young girl living during the Holocaust. The account asks the question, "what if a little girl during the Holocaust had Instagram?" Its innovative use of technology and personal point of view is deeply affecting, and the series has won awards. You don't have to put in the same amount of work as a feature film into your social media stories, but they can still be a very effective part of your promotion strategy.

Type: Regular Technique

Time Required: 5-15 minutes

Podcast Level: Any

How to Do It

If you use Instagram, you can click on your account's icon to post a story. The post gives you options to take a photo or video, or to create text posts with different coloured backgrounds. You can add text to your images or video as well. Instagram works when you use the app; otherwise you can just view posts.

On Facebook, any of your posts can be added to your "story." Each post gives you the option to publish it to your News Feed, but you can publicly post it as a story as well.

Facebook owns Instagram, so many of their features overlap. You can link your Facebook account with your Instagram account, so your story posts on one will show up on the other, and vice versa. This can save you some time.

When you create an Instagram story, in the Create menu, you can add some interactive features, such as a simple poll, a donation button, and a countdown clock. These can be fun ways to let your audience interact with your posts. Bear in mind, these will disappear from Instagram within 24 hours, but you'll still be able to archive them.

Task List:

☐ If you don't have an Instagram or Facebook account, create one.

☐ On Instagram, try clicking on your icon and post a story.

☐ Slide the options at the bottom from right to left, to see different story types.

☐ Try out the features for modifying each post, such as adding text.

☐ Try the "Create" option, and then scroll through the different types of stories you can make.

☐ Try using the "Add To Story" option on Facebook.

☐ Try making polls, or asking questions of your followers.

☐ If you have a new episode or an important milestone coming up, post the countdown clock story to generate interest.

☐ Share photos of your recording process, or visual inspiration for your show's content.

☐ If your show is about a topic which can benefit from a visual element, share it on Instagram.

Related to: Ask Your Whole Audience, Organic Social Media, Posting Video

Further Reading:

- Promote Your Podcast with Instagram

  > thepodcasthost.com/instagram

6. Compile & Share an Ebook

When you've published a decent amount of episodes, you might consider re-writing your scripts and notes from each one into an ebook. You can give this away as an incentive to people who contribute to you through a fundraising campaign, or as a reward for signing up for your mailing list. You can even publish it and offer it for sale through Amazon's self-publishing channels. It's a good way to encapsulate your information, while also rewarding your audience for their commitment.

Type: Big Strategy

Time Required: One month to plan, compile, re-write, and publish

Podcast Level: At least 10 episodes

How to Do It

So, you have a basic script of talking points for each episode (or, better yet, you have transcripts). You have your show notes, and you also have any blog posts or visual aids. You also have an audience that's interested in your show's topic.

For each episode, put together any notes or talking points you used, your transcript if you have one, any visual aids that you might have posted on your website or Instagram, and your show notes and blog post for the episode.

Look at this information as a whole. What's the cohesive narrative? What did you learn about your podcast's topic, as you went through the process of making this podcast? What have you learned about it from your audience and your guests? This is a good time for you to encapsulate what you've learned so far, and what you can share with others.

Edit this information into one cohesive document. A reasonable ebook usually runs about 7,000 to 10,000 words. As long as you're covering the most important points in your information, explaining them clearly, and giving your audience value, length doesn't matter.

It's always a good idea to have someone unbiased and skilled proofread your document before sending it anywhere. You can find someone who does book editing services on Fiverr, or trade services with a friend. A good designer can make sure your ebook is pleasing to the eye and enjoyable to read. If you prefer the DIY route, you can make a pretty good book cover in Canva.

You can save this as one PDF, and give it to your supporters directly. This makes a great gift for the people who have supported you, as well as a good enticement for a new audience.

You can also publish it through Amazon's Kindle Direct Publishing. This lets you set the price, earn royalties, and publish in either digital or paperback.

Task List:

☐ Organize your show notes, scripts/talking points, transcripts, visual aids, and blog posts for each episode.

☐ Take note of what you've learned through this process.

☐ Write a book, using the information you've compiled.

☐ Get an unbiased, skilled editor to proofread and edit your book.

☐ Have a designer make sure your fonts and layout look good, and design a quality cover.

☐ Share this book with your supporters.

Related to: Helping Others To Help Yourself, Enabling Your Existing Audience

Further reading:

• How To Make Great Podcast Art

> thepodcasthost.com/coverart

Advertising Your Podcast

"Many a small thing has been made large by the right kind of advertising."- Mark Twain

The concept of advertising really needs no introduction. This is an ancient and traditional way of promoting a product or service. The concept is quite simple - you pay some money, and you get your ad in front of a particular audience.

If you're open to the idea of running an ad campaign or two, then there are a few good options for podcasters. That's the purpose of this chapter. So, read on, and see if anything jumps out to you...

1. **Overcast Ads**

2. **Podcast Addict Ads**

3. **Pocket Casts Ads**

4. **Print Magazines**

5. **Podnews Advertising**

6. **Paid Facebook Ads**

7. **Advertising on Spotify**

8. **Advertising on Reddit**

9. **Google Ads**

10. Finding Other Ad Spots in Your Niche

11. Email Newsletter Sponsorship

12. Flyers

13. Event Sponsorship

1. Overcast Ads

Overcast is one of the most popular podcast listening apps in the world today. And with good reason – it's a superb app, packed with useful features.

Overcast is built for podcast listeners. But, they also provide the tools for podcasters to advertise their shows in the app. These ads appear as unobtrusive little banners, which the app's users see at the bottom of their screen.

On these banner ads, you'll see a podcast's name, cover art, and a little snippet description tempting the listener to click it.

With Overcast ads, 100% of the folks that you reach are podcast listeners. That's why they're looking at Overcast when they see your ad. They're likely either listening to a podcast, or about to hit play on one.

This means they're literally one click away from browsing your podcast inside their chosen listening app. And one more click away from hitting Play or Subscribe.

There's no education needed here. There's no "what is a podcast?", no "find us at…". It's simply down to the snippet you write when you create your ad.

The ads are unobtrusive, yet clearly visible to the user.

Costs vary on topic, and on demand, but you can usually start advertising on Overcast from around $90.

Type: Short Task

Time Required: 15 minutes to set up. Runs for 1 month.

Podcast Level: 3 episodes or more.

How to Do It

You need to sign up for an Overcast account at Overcast.fm.

Overcast is an iOS-only listening app, but anyone can sign up for an account on their computer.

Once you're in, go to overcast.fm/ads where you'll see the full details. This includes info on current pricing and estimated reach.

As you'll see, ads are broken out into different categories. Naturally, the cost is higher for the more popular ones. You can see how many slots are available, and which ones are currently sold out. If it's one of the sold out ones you're after, you can ask to be notified when they become available.

Once you select a category, you'll click through to a page where you can customise your snippet. You'll want to write a sentence or two that acts as a 'hook', to be displayed alongside the podcast name and cover art.

If you leave this blank, Overcast will use the start of the description in your feed. It's much better to write something in there that doesn't cut off. Try adding "Click here to get started", if you have the room.

Then, you can preview your ad, before reviewing your purchase, and making the payment. It's really simple.

Task List

☐ Sign up for an Overcast account at Overcast.fm.

☐ Select your targeted podcast category.

☐ Customise your snippet.

☐ Preview your ad.

☐ Complete your purchase.

Further Reading:

• Promoting Your Podcast on Overcast

> thepodcasthost.com/overcast

2. Podcast Addict Ads

Podcast Addict is another of the biggest listening apps in the world. Recently, Podcast Addict created a podcast advertising feature.

Type: Short Task

Time Required: 15 minutes to set up. Runs for 1 month.

Podcast Level: 3 episodes or more.

How to Do It

Podcast Addict's ad setup is similar to Overcast in many ways, in terms of how it works, and its benefits.

One slight difference is that there are 2 different ad placements available. You can opt for the main screen – the area where users are searching for new podcasts. Or, you can place your ad in a specific category to target users browsing in there.

You can run your podcast ad in any language. Once live, it will run for a full month.

Task List:

☐ Go to PodcastAddict.com/ads

☐ Enter your show's RSS feed link

☐ Select your advertising plan

☐ Pay

Further Reading:

• Promote Your Podcast on Podcast Addict

> thepodcasthost.com/podcastaddictads

3. Pocket Casts Ads

A third addition to your podcast listening app ad options. The Pocket Casts app is available on iOS, Android, or Desktop, so you have a huge potential reach here.

Type: Short Task

Time Required: 15 minutes to set up. Runs for 1 month.

Podcast Level: 3 episodes or more.

How to Do It

Pocket Casts has a 'Discover' section, where you can run paid placements. This section gets 350k unique views per week, according to the app's creators. Another stat they provide is that their average user listening time is 10 hours per week.

You need to have at least 2 published 'episodes' to run Pocket Casts ads. This includes trailers or Episode Zeros, but shows with no published content will be automatically rejected.

Sponsored slots on Pocket Casts costs a cool $2000. Your show will be displayed prominently in the 'Discover' section for one week.

This option looks suited to big brand or network shows who're short on time, but have a bit of budget behind them to help grow that early core audience.

Task List:

☐ Go to pocketcasts.com/paid-placements

☐ Request a paid placement

4. Print Magazines

Are you podcasting in a traditionally "non-techy" niche? Maybe you spend quite a lot of time explaining what a podcast is to your target audience.

If this is you, then the best route for running paid ads might be through industry or trade magazines.

Print magazines have experienced a bit of a renaissance in recent years. In fact, it seems to be the ultra-niche ones that have best weathered the digital storm, and continue to grow from strength to strength.

So if there's a thriving magazine based around your podcast topic, why not consider advertising there?

This is perfect for doing some targeted advertising for your show. Whether you're podcasting about fly fishing, gardening, or model railways, you'll likely find a magazine serving up the same topic to a dedicated fanbase.

The best thing is, if someone's going out of their way to buy a mag, they're already fanatical about this topic, and so they're likely to be super-interested in finding more content about it.

Most, if not all magazines have ads in them. But, some magazines might also be open to a sponsored content, or guest article partnership. Here, you can write a piece for them that's useful and interesting to their readers, but also directs them back to your show.

Type: Big Strategy

Time Required: Typically a one month turnaround. It depends a lot on the magazine's publishing frequency.

Podcast Level: 5 episodes or more.

How to Do It

Finding a Magazine

Firstly, identify the magazine you'd like to try your advertising experiment. If you're not familiar with one already, the easiest way to do this would be a Google search. For example "best model railway magazines", or "miniature wargaming magazines".

You could also simply browse the magazines in your local newsagent, and see if there's anything that fits the bill.

Look for an advertising contact. This will usually be an email address on one of the first pages, next to the editorial. If you're on the magazines website, you should find it on their contact page.

Reach out to them to ask about their reach, pricing, and availability. You could enquire about writing a sponsored or guest article for them too, if this interests you.

Ask for details on ad sizes, placing, and general guidelines. Also, ask if their service involves a graphic design option. If not, you might want to hire someone on a platform like Fiverr.

Pro Tip: magazines often offer discounts for first time advertisers, to test the waters. They also sometimes offer cut-price rates if they have space free close to a deadline. So, if you can book last minute, it's worth asking for the discount. Let them know you're willing to remain flexible, and fill a gap for them, when they need it, in exchange for a lower fee.

Creating Your Ad

Depending on your niche, you might still have to dedicate a bit of space in your ad to the "what is a podcast?" question. Just be sure to really sell them on the benefits of listening, and stress that it's absolutely free.

You might even want to send them to a dedicated 'how to listen to a podcast' page on your site, for maximum effect.

Your ad - like any type of content - will sink or swim based on its headline. You might want to avoid your headline simply being your podcast name, and opt instead for a compelling question. Something that will strike a chord with your target audience. What will make them want to check out your solution?

For example - "Worried about your dog's weight?" - a pet health podcast. Or, "7 natural fertilizers you didn't know about" - a gardening podcast. This headline then leads into the fact that you've discussed it in detail on your show, which they can find now, for free, at your-website-dot-com.

Task List:

☐ Identify the magazine you'd like to advertise in.

☐ Reach out to their advertising or sales department.

☐ Get details on pricing, placement, and general guidelines.

☐ Choose a compelling headline - sell the benefits of listening.

☐ Create ad, either with the magazine or with your own designer.

5. Podnews Advertising

Podnews is an essential daily email newsletter. It's predominantly aimed at keeping podcasters up-to-date with the latest industry news. But, most podcasters are podcast listeners too, and you can advertise your podcast to them here for $29 a day.

With Podnews advertising, you can promote your show to over 16,000 subscribers every weekday. Recipients include folks from the likes of the BBC, NPR, Gimlet, and Apple Podcasts – you never know who might take an interest.

The ads appear right in the middle of the main content, as a seperate box, under the heading 'Classifieds'. Each ad is a hyperlinked headline, and a 30-40 word description.

All ads that are run in Podnews will also appear permanently on their website, and within their daily companion podcast episode shownotes.

You can sponsor the Podnews newsletter on a monthly basis. This includes a logo at the top of the newsletter and varying text messaging throughout the month. They also offer other sponsorship options too, including bespoke solutions.

You can get your logo on Podnews every day by becoming a silver supporter on Patreon for as little as $50 a month. Logos appear in a random order every day, though the higher your level of support, the higher your logo goes too.

Type: Short Task

Time Required: 20 minutes

Podcast Level: 5 episodes or more.

How to Do It

Classified ads in podnews.net start at US$29 a day. You simply register at podnews.net/classifieds, write your ad (30-40 words) and headline.

Choose the dates you want to run it, and pay.

Alternatively, you can contact the Podnews Head of Sales, at sales@podnews.net if you're interested in monthly, silver, or bespoke sponsorship.

Task List:

☐ Write your ad.

☐ Choose the dates you want to run it.

☐ Pay online.

6. Paid Facebook Ads

Facebook! Love it or hate it, it commands the attention of billions of people, worldwide.

If you're a Facebook user, then running a few paid ads on the platform might be worth considering.

Facebook is so widely used, it's likely your target audience are already on there, in some way, shape, or form.

A paid Facebook ad can stick you on the screen right in front of their eyes. In this task, we'll run you through some best practices for maximising your results.

Type: Big Strategy

Time Required: 15mins to set up. Runs for as long as you like.

Podcast Level: 5 episodes or more.

How to Do It

You can run targeted ads on Facebook. Targeting helps focus the types of people you're looking to reach. That means you can spend less money, and reach more relevant listeners.

For example, we could advertise our space show – *Hostile Worlds* – on Facebook this way. We might target users who have listed an interest in Space or Astronomy, or who are members of a 'space chat' group, or have liked 'Astronomy Today' magazine.

Facebook is a busy platform, and, with a good advert and the right targeting, it isn't too difficult to rack up a few 'likes'. But, these don't always translate to listens. In fact, there's no guarantee the folks you'll reach with your ads are podcast listeners – or even know what a podcast is.

That's where a second layer of targeting fits. Target those who like BOTH space AND podcasting. Then, you'll reach folks who are more likely to listen. This cuts your reach, of course, but makes it more relevant. That said, I definitely think there are advantages to reaching outside of our already crowded 'existing listeners' pool, so don't rule out that strategy either.

The most important factor of all though, is your actual ad. You can totally nail the targeting, but if your ad doesn't compell your target audience, this will be a waste of your money.

Creating Your Ad

There's little point in publishing a full episode as your ad. Getting someone to consume an entire podcast episode on Facebook is going to be near enough impossible. Instead, we want to cut the podcast up and create micro-content from it. If you film your podcast, this step is going to be much easier (and more powerful) for you.

You do this by finding a 1-2 minute segment within the full episode that's particularly interesting or entertaining. If you edit it to include captions, that video becomes a piece of content on its own.

I suggest creating 2-3 pieces of micro content from each one of your podcast episodes. You can use these across all the different social media platforms. The result is a much more engaging post, rather than a boring "listen to my latest episode.... Boringtweet.com" type post.

If you don't have any video recordings, then you can use tools like *Headliner* to create nice audiograms of your podcast. This strategy will still work with audiograms, but it's likely to be less effective, as audiograms aren't quite as engaging.

Publish your micro content as an organic post on your Facebook feed. This allows you to gather some engagement before you put any advertising spend behind it. The purpose of the text in your post is to hook people into watching the video. The purpose of the video is to hook people into clicking the link to listen to the full show.

Once your micro content is out there, give it around 24 hours to distribute itself out into the world. Once it's done that, you can head into your Facebook ads manager, create your targeted campaign, and start getting in front of loads of new potential listeners!

Task List:

☐ Create micro content from the episode you want to promote.

☐ Publish it firstly as an organic post.

☐ Give the post around 24 hours.

☐ Go to Facebook ads manager to create your campaign.

☐ Choose 'traffic' as your objective.

☐ Select your audience targeting.

☐ Begin your campaign.

Related to: other techniques/strategies that work well with this.

Further Reading:

• How to Grow Your Podcast with Facebook Ads

> thepodcasthost.com/facebookads

• A Beginners' Guide to Audiograms

> thepodcasthost.com/audiograms

7. Advertising on Spotify

Spotify have invested big in podcasting these past few years. They've also cemented their position as the number two place podcasts are consumed, behind Apple themselves.

Spotify is still predominantly a music platform, and most users will be using it purely to listen to music. But there are certainly far worse places to advertise your podcast. Currently, the app boasts a whopping 116 million "ad supported" listeners. These are folks who obviously enjoy listening to audio.

Spotify ads are predominantly audio, though there's a visual element too. They display your logo on screen with a "Learn More" button, whilst the ad is playing.

The ads are played in-between songs or podcast episodes, to listeners who use Spotify on their free tier.

Type: Big Strategy

Time Required: 2-3 days

Podcast Level: 20 episodes or more.

How to Do It

You can create and run a 30 second audio ad for your show by signing up to Spotify Ad Studio, at https://adstudio.spotify.com

Here, you can really hone in on the targeting, selecting things like age, gender, location, and even the styles of music your ads will appear alongside.

Spotify ads are similar to social media ads in the sense that you set a budget and date range, before being offered an estimated number of ads to be served. For example, $500 might get you around 25,000 ads.

This is better than social media, in the sense that you're reaching people who are actively consuming audio content. And if they happen to be looking at their screen at the time the ad is playing, they'll also see your ad logo and a "Learn More" button, which will take them to your destination of choice.

Creating Your Ad

You can create your own ad, or work with Spotify to have them create it for you.

Spotify provides audio and image specs for ads you want to make yourself. Or, they offer a Voiceover Tool service for ad buyers at no extra cost.

With the Voiceover Tool, you write your script, select the ad language, choose a preferred voice type to read your ad, and you can choose background music from their extensive library too.

Spotify will then have the ad recorded and mixed. It'll be ready to review within 24-48 hours, after which, you'll have the option to approve it, make changes, or reject it.

Once approved, your ad is ready to be heard.

8. Here Are Spotify's Ad Guidelines

Meet your audience where they are

Your listeners will hear your message between songs during their listening session. If you choose to use background music, consider using similar music to your audience's listening preferences.

Know your listeners

Ads that are personalized to the listener see higher engagement. Consider including a targeted approach to your messaging. For instance, if targeting New York, say, "Hey, New York!"

Get to the point

Take advantage of the first few seconds to introduce yourself, your business, and the purpose of your ad.

Include a call to action

Ads that have a direct call-to-action have clickthrough rates that are ~3x higher than those with none. Ask the listener to do something (such as "tap to find a location") and they'll be more likely to engage with your ad.

Be clear and stay on message

Focus on the most important point you want the listener to walk away with. Try to avoid skits, jokes or testimonials that make it difficult for listeners to connect with your brand.

Communicate benefits

Talk about exclusives, sales or promotional codes in your audio ad.

Keep a consistent tone and tempo

For a 30 second ad, aim for between 55-75 words and try to keep your pace even throughout.

Task List:

☐ Sign up at adstudio.spotify.com.

☐ Use their guidelines to make your ad. OR, work with them to create it.

☐ Select the listener types you want to target.

☐ Select your budget.

☐ Select your date range.

☐ Submit and/or approve your ad.

9. Advertising on Reddit

Reddit is described as a "social news aggregation, web content rating, and discussion website." On top of that, it's one of the most visited websites in the world – and it's yet another place you can run paid ads to promote your content.

Type: Short Task

Time Required: 15 minutes to set up. Runs for as long as you like.

Podcast Level: 3 episodes or more.

How to Do It

To advertise your podcast on Reddit, you first need to sign up with Reddit Ads. You can then look at creating your first campaign.

Here, Reddit will ask you for your campaign objective. The options they give include "Brand Awareness and Reach", "Traffic", "Conversions", and "Video Views".

You can tailor your ad targeting, going as wide or as narrow as you like, selecting from a range of interests and niche Reddit communities.

You can also run location targeting. If you're based in the US, you can even do this on a per-state basis. On top of that, you can choose which devices your ads will run on – for example, a podcast about iOS/Apple products wouldn't want to waste their money advertising to Android users.

One interesting aspect of Reddit ads is that you can upload video as your promoted content. This gives you the opportunity to use a compelling section of one of your episodes, re-worked in video format. For podcasters, this has the potential to work really well.

Task List:

☐ Go to to redditinc.com/advertising.

215

☐ Sign up.

☐ Create your campaign.

☐ Target your audience.

☐ Set your budget and timeframe.

10. Google Ads

Google ads is another behemoth of online advertising, and there's a good chance you see dozens of these every single day.

Most search terms will turn up a handful of ads at the very top of the page. You can spot these because they have the "Ad" text beside them.

If you have a show which answers a question, in any way, then Google ads could work really well for you. For example, you're a coach that teaches people how to be more confident on your show, or you're a running influencer who tells people what are the best running products to buy.

If you know what people are searching for in your niche, and your show has an answer for that search, then you can use Google ads.

They may not be *quite* as effective as organic content. But getting anything to the very top of a Google search result can be challenging, and takes a bit of time.

By all means, work on optimising your organic content for search. But in the meantime, putting some money behind a Google Ad or two can give you a nice boost in traffic to your site - and downloads to your podcast!

Type: Short task

Time Required: 15mins to set up. Runs for as long as you like.

Podcast Level: 5 episodes or more.

How to Do It

Google ads are 'text only', which is a benefit for many people.

Firstly, it means it's quick. You can have a campaign up and running in just 20 minutes. All you have to do is write. No pesky image or video creating.

Next, it means that anyone can compete on an even playing field, no matter your budget. In contrast, on Facebook and Instagram, it's often those with the biggest budget that win. The big companies can spend more on amazingly designed image adverts, or pro video content.

On Google ads, though, it's about your message, and that alone. So, if you know the words people are typing into Google, and what they really want as a result, you can hook them in with a nicely crafted message.

For example, we might choose to advertise our 'how to podcast' show, *Podcraft*. I know that one question it answers well is: "How do I start a podcast?" So, I think of the terms related to that. For example:

- how to start a podcast

- how to make a podcast

- how to create a podcast

I create one ad-set (a Google ads term that just means a collection of adverts) that targets all of those keywords together.

Then, I create a headline and a subheader for my ad that answers the question those searchers have. Such as:

- Learn How to Start a Podcast

- Podcraft's Step by Step Guide

Finally, you can give a bit more detail in the description.

Podcraft is a podcast that teaches you everything you need to know about starting your own show. Listen as Colin & Matthew break it down, as if you were a 5 year old!

You can run Google ads for as little as $1 (or less!) per day, just to try it out. Even at that level, you should be able to grow awareness, bit by bit. Just like social, it'll take a little testing to find the right keywords, and the right message. Once you've found it, you can ramp it up and capitalise on that success.

Task List:

☐ Investigate the questions and search terms your target listener is seeking out.

☐ Choose your keywords/keyphrases to target.

☐ Decide where you'd like to point your traffic to.

☐ Set your budget.

11. Finding Other Ad Spots in Your Niche

It's possible to advertise on a wide variety of different platforms online. Most groups or sites focused around a common audience or topic will have the option to buy ads.

Your potential options will range from websites, to social groups, and forums. You can even run advertising on Linkedin if you think it'll be relevant to your topic, and target audience.

Type: Short Task

Time Required: 2-3 hours

Podcast Level: 5 episodes or more.

How to Do It

Firstly, identify the site or platform you'd like to run ads on. You might already have somewhere in mind - perhaps a site or community that you already visit regularly - or, you might try a Google search to find sites that perform well.

Most sites you visit will run things like banner ads. If these are specific to the site's overall topic, then you could reach out to the webmaster and ask for more details. This will be things like pricing, as well as estimated clicks, tracking options, and any other analytics they might offer.

An example of this would be TheWarGamesWebsite.com, where you'll find banner ads linking to companies who design and sculpt miniatures. These ads appear the same to every person who visits the site, but given they are on the site at all suggests they'll likely be interested in them.

Some other websites you visit will run ads, but they'll be based on the cookies of each unique visitor. This will be obvious to you when looking at the ads on a site.

Task List:

☐ Identify some sites and platforms in your niche.

☐ Review them to find out if they run ads.

☐ Contact the webmaster or owner to ask about pricing and analytics.

12. Email Newsletter Sponsorship

Email is still the often overlooked king of online communication. Websites and social media platforms may come and go, but every single person who uses the internet has an email address.

Email newsletters are also still arguably the most effective way for brands and businesses to keep their fans up-to-date. And many of these brands and businesses will offer sponsorship opportunities for their newsletters, too. This can be an excellent way to get in front of your target audience.

Type: Short Task

Time Required: 2-3 hours

Podcast Level: 5 episodes or more.

How to Do It

A good starting point is to consider the email newsletters in your show's niche that you're already signed up to. Do any of these have ongoing ad or sponsorship slots?

If so, it'll be possible to get details on pricing and availability, either on their main website, or by contacting the person (or people) behind it.

As always, your advert will sink or swim based on how compelling you make it. The best performing ads are the ones that present a solution to a problem, or ask a question that the reader is already asking themselves.

- "Worried about your dog's weight?"

- "6 ways to help your kids build healthy habits"

- "Struggling to keep on top of your home repairs?"

It's all totally topic and niche dependent. The bottom line though is that you'll link back to an individual episode which is all about the question or point you've just raised. It might even be the title of the episode itself.

How your ad displays will vary from newsletter to newsletter. Commonly though, they'll be text ads with 30-50 word snippets. You might want to mention in the ad that it's a podcast, and also that it's free. Use wording like "listen for free, at…", or "listen and subscribe for free!".

Task List:

☐ Identify some email newsletters in your niche.

☐ Review them to find out if they run ads.

☐ Contact the business or owner to ask about pricing and analytics.

☐ Base your ad around an individual episode - present a solution to a relatable problem.

13. Flyers

Paper or card flyers are one of the oldest marketing tools out there. And even in this age of social media and digital communication, we still see them everywhere. You'll no doubt regularly get them through your door, see them scattered on tables, or pinned to community noticeboards.

Using flyers to advertise your podcast can be an effective marketing strategy, if done correctly. They can get your show in front of potential listeners in an eye-catching and tangible way. They can tempt these potential listeners into finding out more, by offering a clear problem-solution relevant to your content.

Type: Big Strategy

Time Required: One week

Podcast Level: 5 episodes or more.

How to Do It

Before you even decide what to put on your flyer, you should think about what you're actually going to do with them. Who are the ideal listeners and target audience that you want to reach, and where do they hang out?

For example, if you do a niche podcast about beekeeping, or cheesemaking, there's no point putting 5000 flyers through the door of every house in your community. But if your podcast was actually all *about* your local community, then this would be one of the best uses of them.

Podcasting about sport or fitness? Try public tables or noticeboards at your local leisure centre or health club.

Perhaps your show is focussed on shopping or fashion? In which case, maybe handing them out on your local high street or shopping centre might be the best approach. This has the added bonus of letting you actually chat to people too.

Noticeboards at train stations also have an added bonus of giving commuters some new listening to pass the time.

Once you've decided what you're going to do with your flyers, you need to think about design. The same rules apply for any type of advert. A clear and compelling title that encourages people to find out more, and a call to action that directs them back to your website.

This is where you can present a solution to a problem your target listener will likely relate to. One that's covered in the podcast itself.

As ever, it's totally topic and audience dependent. It can be anything from "Tired of Yo-Yo Dieting?", to "How to save for your dream holiday!".

Use both sides of the flyer to take full advantage of the space. But don't pack it full of text. The flyer should simply be a lead back to your website, where you can then drive subscribers to your show, or direct them into your funnel.

Opt for a clean, skimmable design with some nice illustrations to break it up. Have your podcast's name on there, but not as the main heading. And have your domain name on there a few times too, to make sure they only have one place they need to go.

You can hire a designer to create your flyer for you. If you don't already work with a designer, then you'll find lots of freelancers on Fiverr. Or, you could do it yourselves for free, on a platform like canva.com.

You will still need to have them printed, and there's plenty of services that can do this for you, both online and offline. It's always cheaper (per flyer) to buy more, so it might be worth considering doing one that is evergreen, and not time sensitive.

Task List:

☐ Decide where you'd like to use flyers to promote your podcast. Who are you looking to reach?

☐ Draft up your flyer's content. Who are your target audience? How will you tempt them to read on?

☐ Drive them to your website where you can then fully control the next stage of their journey.

☐ Use a designer, or create the flyer yourself on canva.com.

☐ Don't pack your flyer with blocks of text. Make it easily skimmable.

☐ Avoid time-sensitive content on your flyer if you are buying in a large bulk.

☐ Decide on a local or online printing service.

Related to: Guerrilla Marketing

14. Event Sponsorship

Most topics and niches have events centered around them. Typically, these will be in the form of conferences and conventions.

It's common for these events to be sponsored by companies and businesses in and around their niche too. This can be a great way to advertise your podcast in front of your target audience.

Type: Big Strategy

Time Required: Several months prior to event to agree on sponsorship

Podcast Level: 10 episodes or more.

How to Do It

Event organisers will tend to offer different sponsorship tiers. There's usually a main event sponsor, though depending on the niche, this could be pretty expensive.

Sponsorship of things like lanyards and canvas bags though, can be a lot cheaper, and pretty effective at the same time.

With the lanyards, there are eyes going to them the whole day as people meet, and look at each other's name.

With bags, these are carried around the whole day and are constantly on display as attendees fill them full of swag.

Both the lanyards and the bags are generally kept by attendees too, so there's a good chance your branding will make it back to their own home afterwards.

The beauty of event sponsorship is that you don't even physically need to be there. You can sponsor an event on the other side of the world, or multiple events at the same time!

Remember that a lanyard or bag needs more than simply a logo to be effective. You'll definitely want your URL on there too, and a one-liner to temp folks into checking it out.

For example, we have sponsored lanyards in the past. Here are 2 examples of what we put on them.

- Alitu, The Podcast Maker - The quick & easy way to make your podcast

- The Podcast Host - The best 'How to Podcast' resource on the web

Task List:

☐ Draw up a list of conferences and conventions in your podcast's niche.

☐ Look for sponsorship info on each one's website.

☐ Decide on which available sponsorship tier you'd like to opt for.

☐ Ask about their design criteria.

☐ Ask for examples of previous designs.

☐ Create your design along with a hook or tagline to direct people back to your website.

Related to: Flyers

The End

(Welcome to the Beginning!)

There are enough tactics and strategies in this book to keep you busy for the next few years. As we said at the start, it's not about trying to do them all at once. It's about choosing the select few you think are a great fit for your content and your audience, then throwing your full weight and attention behind trying to make them work.

We're assuming you've reached the end of the book because you've had a read-through, as opposed to actually doing each task one after the other. If it's the latter though, you've completed the game - well done! Go and book yourself a fortnight in the Bahamas and have a well-earned rest.

If you're a mere mortal like the rest of us though, the work is only just beginning. The next step is to create your own unique podcast growth plan strategy, and plan out the next 12 months and beyond.

As a companion to this book, we've created a handy chart for you to print out and pin on your wall - you can grab it at

ThePodcastHost.com/AudienceGrowthBook

We can't thank you enough for picking up a copy of the book. We've been putting out "how to" content and resources on ThePodcastHost.com since 2011, and it has become one of the biggest resources of its kind on the web today.

Podcast promotion is just one area that we cover on the site. We have over 600 articles published on everything from choosing a mic and learning to edit, to establishing yourself as an authority and earning a crust from your show.

That said, the question of "how can I grow my audience?" comes up time and time again, which is why we thought it'd be a great idea to stick every tip, tactic, and strategy we know into one handy book.

If you've enjoyed and found value in it, we'd be extremely grateful if you could leave a review on whatever platform you use, or wherever you bought it.

You can tag us on Twitter too, at @thepodcasthost, using the hashtag #PodcastGrowthBook.

We'd also love to work with you in The Podcast Host Academy. That's our membership site, where you'll get access to all our courses, downloadable resources, and weekly live Q&A sessions. Find it at ThePodcastHost.com/Academy.

Finally, if you'd like to save time on editing and production so that you can focus on working through this book, be sure to check out Alitu.com.

Alitu is our 'Podcast Maker' web app that helps you create and publish your podcast in a quick and pain-free manner. Sign up for a free 7-day trial and give it a spin. We're certain you'll love it!

Cheers,

The Podcast Host Team (Colin, Matthew, & Lindsay)

Printed in Great Britain
by Amazon